Beginner's
Icelandic

with 2 Audio CDs

HIPPOCRENE BEGINNER'S SERIES

ARABIC
ARMENIAN
ASSYRIAN
BASQUE WITH 2 AUDIO CDs
BULGARIAN WITH 2 AUDIO CDs
CHINESE WITH 2 AUDIO CDs
CROATIAN WITH 2 AUDIO CDs
CZECH WITH 2 AUDIO CDs
DANISH WITH 2 AUDIO CDs
DARI WITH AUDIO CD
DUTCH
FINNISH WITH 2 AUDIO CDs
GAELIC
GEORGIAN WITH 2 AUDIO CDs
GREEK WITH 2 AUDIO CDs
HUNGARIAN WITH 2 AUDIO CDs
IRAQI ARABIC WITH 2 AUDIO CDs
IRISH WITH AUDIO CD
ITALIAN
JAPANESE WITH 2 AUDIO CDs
KOREAN WITH 2 AUDIO CDs
LADINO WITH 2 AUDIO CDs
LITHUANIAN
MAORI
NORWEGIAN WITH 2 AUDIO CDs
PERSIAN
POLISH WITH 2 AUDIO CDs
RUSSIAN
SERBIAN WITH 2 AUDIO CDs
SHONA
SICILIAN
SPANISH
SWEDISH WITH 2 AUDIO CDs
TURKISH
VIETNAMESE
WELSH WITH 2 AUDIO CDs
YORUBA WITH 2 AUDIO CDs

BEGINNER'S
Icelandic

WITH 2 AUDIO CDS

Helga Hilmisdóttir
and
Jacek Kozlowski

HIPPOCRENE BOOKS, INC.
New York

For information, address:
HIPPOCRENE BOOKS, INC.
171 Madison Avenue
New York, NY 10016
www.hippocrenebooks.com

Library of Congress Cataloging-in-Publication Data

Hilmisdóttir, Helga.
Beginner's Icelandic : with 2 audio CDs / Helga Hilmisdóttir and Jacek
Kozlowski.
    p. cm. — (Hippocrene beginner's series)
English and Icelandic.
ISBN 978-0-7818-1191-0
    1. Icelandic language—Textbooks for foreign speakers—English.
    2. Icelandic language—Self-instruction. I. Kozlowski, Jacek. II. Title.

PD2413.H55 2007
439'.6983421—dc22

                                                            2007017780

Printed in the United States of America.

TABLE OF CONTENTS

INTRODUCTION

People

Icelandic is the language of Iceland, a European island nation in the North Atlantic. It is a Nordic country and thus shares cultural and political ties with the Faroe Islands, Denmark, Norway, Sweden, Finland, and Greenland. Icelandic is a Germanic language, and so it is related to the Scandinavian languages as well as English and German.

As of January 2007, Iceland had approximately 300,000 inhabitants of which approximately 190,000 or 65 percent lived in the capital city Reykjavik and its surrounding areas. The country's population rose by 2.2 percent in 2005. The overall population density is the lowest in Europe with only three inhabitants per square kilometer. The inner, mountainous, and glacial part of the country is not inhabited, and most populations are around the coastal regions.

The only city in Iceland is Reykjavik. The only urban area outside of the capital is Akureyri which has approximately 15,000 inhabitants. Other towns are considerably smaller. Iceland is divided into 23 counties (**sýsla**). Within these counties there are 98 municipalities (**sveitarfélag**).

Icelandic Names

Icelanders use a naming convention whereby the father's or mother's first name is combined with the words for *son* or *daughter* (**son** or **dóttir**) to form a second name. Thus, the singer Björk's full name is Björk Guðmundsdóttir, which literally translates to *Björk, daughter of Guðmundur*. This might seem a bit strange to English speakers and other foreigners, since it means that siblings often don't have the same last names. Björk's brother, for example, would have Guðmundsson as a second name. To make things more complex, different generations have different last names since fathers and grandfathers don't have the same first names. Thus, if your grandfather's name were Jón, your father would have Jónsson as a second name, and if your father's first name were Steingrímur, your last name would be Steingrímsson or Steingrímsdóttir. People are listed in the phone book by their first names.

Geography

Iceland is 103,000 square kilometers in area of which 11.5 percent is covered by glaciers. It contains the largest glacier in Europe, **Vatnajökull**. **Vatnajökull** reaches a thickness of 1,000 meters at its thickest point. In recent years, many of the glaciers have been retreating. Iceland is a geologically young country with many active volcanoes, and earthquakes are common. For example, Surtsey Island in the south part of the country was born just a few decades ago from an undersea volcanic eruption.

The country has a very small amount of wood and trees. In recent years, Icelanders have put a great deal of effort into planting new trees.

Climate

Iceland experiences a typically maritime climate which is quite mild because of the influence of the Gulf Stream. The annual average temperature in Iceland is approximately 5°C or 41°F. The weather changes rapidly and it is recommended to bring warm clothes when travelling to Iceland, even in the summer.

Due to Iceland's northern position, the days are very long in the summer and very short in the winter. The Midnight Sun can be seen for approximately ten weeks in the summer months. From mid-November to the end of January, daylight lasts for only three to four hours.

The northern lights are often seen in Iceland, especially in rural parts of the island.

History

Iceland was settled in 874 A.D. and adopted Christianity in the year 1000. In 930, Iceland formed the **Alþingi** (*Althingi*), the oldest active parliament in the world. The country lost its independence in 1262 when it was ruled by Norway. In 1387, Danish rule succeeded Norwegian rule, and this lasted until home rule was awarded in 1904 and autonomy in 1918. Iceland was still officially under the Danish king from 1918 to 1944 and became fully independent in 1944 during World War II. In 1949, Iceland became a charter member of NATO. Iceland is a member of the Common Market of the European Union and has signed the European Economic Area agreement but is, as of 2007, not a member of the European Union.

Government

The president is the head of the state. However, the day-to-day role of the president is primarily symbolic in nature. As of this writing, the president of Iceland is Dr. Ólafur Ragnar Grímsson. Icelanders often pride themselves on having elected the first female president in the world, Vigdís Finnbogadóttir, who was elected president in 1980.

All legislative power is exercised by the **Alþingi**, which is elected every four years and consists of 63 members. The five major parties are, from left to right, *The Left-Green movement* (**Vinstrihreyfingin – grænt framboð**), *The Social-Democratic Alliance* (**Samfylkingin**), *The Progressive Party* (**Framsóknarflokkurinn**), *The Liberal Party* (**Frjálslyndi flokkurinn**), and *The Independence Party* (**Sjálfstæðisflokkurinn**).

Economy

In the past, Iceland's economy depended mainly on the fishing industry. This is, to a large extent, still true today, though fishing quotas and declining fish stocks have lessened the importance of the industry as a whole.

Today tourism, entertainment, software production, biotechnology, and financial services are all growing sectors. Most of the country's power is produced from hydro or geothermal sources.

Religion

The state church in Iceland is the Evangelical Lutheran Church. The majority of the population, 92.2 percent, is Evangelical Lutheran, with other Lutherans making up an additional 3.1 percent. Roman Catholics account for 0.9 percent of the population. There is also a Catholic church in Reykjavik and a number of churches for other groups.

Literature and the Arts

Iceland has one of Europe's highest literacy rates, and Icelanders pride themselves on their literary history. The Sagas, prose narratives of historic or legendary figures and events of the heroic age of Norway and Iceland, were written from 1200–1350. A selection of the original manuscripts can be viewed at the Culture House in Reykjavik.

Iceland has had one Nobel Prize winner for literature, Halldór Kiljan Laxness (1902–1998). Among his most acknowledged works are the novels *Independent People* (**Sjálfstætt fólk** 1934–5) and *The Bell of Iceland* (**Íslandsklukkan** 1943–6). Some of his novels have been adapted for the screen, for example *The Atom Station* (**Atómstöðin** 1948) directed by Þorsteinn Jónsson (1984) and *The Honour of the House* (**Ungfrúin góða og húsið**) directed by Guðný Halldórsdóttir (1999).

Guðbergur Bergsson (b. 1932), another renowned Icelandic writer, wrote *The Swan* (**Svanurinn**) in 1991. He has been awarded the Swedish Academy's Nordic Literature Prize, which is one of the most distinguished Nordic awards for literature.

In recent years, there has been a growing interest in Icelandic mysteries. The most successful writer within that genre is Arnaldur Indriðason. An adaptation of his book *Jar City* (**Mýrin** 2000) directed by Baltasar Kormákur was the most popular film in Iceland in 2006. Hallgrímur Helgason is another popular contemporary writer. His best known novel, **101 Reykjavik** (1996), was also made into a film by Baltasar Kormákur (2000).

Iceland has also exported many famous musicians, including Björk, The Sugarcubes, Sigur Rós, Múm, Quarashi, and GusGus. Ari Alexander Magnússon's documentary *Screaming Masterpiece* (**Gargandi snilld** 2005) shows footage from concerts and interviews from some of the most talented musicians in Iceland today.

Iceland has a vibrant cultural scene and it should not be a problem for visitors to find cultural happenings. Events and perfomances are organized by The Icelandic Symphony Orchestra, The Icelandic Opera, The National Art Gallery, The Reykjavik Art Gallery, The Icelandic Dance Corporation, The National Theatre, and by various institutions, museums, galleries, and venues around the country.

Good Luck!

Learning Icelandic is a challenging but rewarding endeavor. If you have the chance to visit Iceland, you will be greeted with an unforgettable experience and an opportunity to practice your language skills. Good luck!

ABBREVIATIONS

Parts of speech and other grammatical terms

acc.	accusative
adj.	adjective
adv.	adverb
comp.	comparative
conj.	conjunction
dat.	dative
def.	definite form
f.	feminine
gen.	genitive
imp.	imperative
interj.	interjection
interr.	interrogative
irr.	irregular
lit.	literally
m.	masculine
n.	noun
neu.	neuter
nom.	nominative
num.	numeral
past	past tense
pers.	person
pl.	plural
poss.	possessive
prep.	preposition
pron.	pronoun
refl.	reflexive
sing.	singular
subj.	subjunctive
super.	superlative
v.	verb

PRONUNCIATION

A note on pronunciation: this book is not meant to be a course on linguistics, so many of the sounds and concepts have been simplified for ease of learning.

The Icelandic Alphabet

The Icelandic alphabet contains 32 letters in the following order:

a á b d ð e é f g h i í j k l m n o ó p r s t u ú v x y ý þ æ ö

In the following chart, the first column contains each letter in its upper-case and lower-case form followed by the way that it is *spelled in Icelandic* in parentheses. The second column gives the approximate pronunciation of each letter, and the third column gives a few examples from Icelandic.

Letters	As in	Icelandic words
A a (a)	f*a*ther	**p*a*bbi, g*a*m*a*ll, b*a*ra** (father, old, only)
Á á (á)	lo*u*d (but with less of a w sound at the end of the diphthong)	**bl*á*r, *á*n, að f*á*** (blue, without, to get)
B b (bé)	*b*ed (but unvoiced, more like a *p*)	***b*ara, að *b*reyta, að *b*era** (only, to change, to carry)
D d (dé)	*d*og (but unvoiced, more like a *t*)	***d*agur, að *d*rekka, *d*æmi** (day, to drink, example)
Ð ð (eð)	*th*is or *th*istle (voiced and unvoiced, never used at the beginning of words)	**ma*ð*ur, bla*ð*, gla*ð*ur** (man, sheet of paper, happy)
E e (e)	l*e*t	**að *e*nda, að b*e*ra, þ*e*tta** (to finish, to carry, this)

7

É é (é)	*ye*s	*é*g, f*é*kk, þ*é*r (I, got, you, *dat.*)
F f (eff)	*f*rom	*f*ram, a*f*tur (forward, again)
	when between vowels or after a vowel, *f* is a *v* sound like a*v*ow	að so*f*a, a*f*i, (to sleep, grandfather)
	when followed by an *l* or an *n, f* is pronounced like the letter *p* (as in *p*ot)	Ke*f*lavík, karta*f*la, sa*f*n, sto*f*na (Keflavík, potato, museum, to establish)
G g (gé)	*g*ood	að *g*era, *g*aman (to do, fun)
	when followed by *t*, *g* sounds like German i*ch* (unvoiced gutteral)	sa*g*t, hæ*g*t, la*g*t (said, slowly, laid)
	when *g* is between vowels or between the letters *r* or *ð*, or when last letter of a word, it becomes a voiced guttural	að la*g*a, sa*g*a, lö*g* (to fix, story, law)
H h (há)	*h*ouse	að *h*afa, *h*ún, á*h*uga (to have, she, interest)
	in the letter combination *hv* the *h* is pronounced like a *k* (as in *k*ite)	*h*ver, *h*vað, *h*var, *h*vernig (who, what, where, how)
I i (i)	t*i*n	að h*i*tta, f*i*skur, yf*i*r (to meet, fish, over)
Í í (í)	s*ee*	*í*s, *í*slenska, *í*þróttir (ice, Icelandic language, sports)
J j (joð)	*y*es	*j*á, að hlæ*j*a, *j*akki (yes, to laugh, jacket)
K k (ká)	*k*ite	*k*a*k*a, *k*anns*k*i, *k*ona (cake, maybe, woman)

L l (ell)	*l*ate	að *l*abba, *l*íf, *l*ist (to walk, life, art)
M m (emm)	*m*ake	að *m*issa, *m*óðir, *m*jólk (to lose, mother, milk)
N n (enn)	*n*ose	*n*úna, *n*ótt, *n*iður (now, night, down)
O o (o)	similar to t*o*ffee	að l*o*fa, *o*któber, að s*o*fa (to promise, October, to sleep)
Ó ó (ó)	l*ow*	bl*ó*m, b*ó*k, að *ó*ska (flower, book, to wish)
P p (pé)	*p*an	að *p*akka, *p*eningur, só*p*ur (to pack, money, broom)
R r (err)	like Spanish *rr*	að *r*aka, *r*úm, á*r* (to shave, bed, year)
S s (ess)	*s*aw	*s*jö, *s*kemmtilegur, *s*kór (seven, fun, shoe)
T t (té)	*t*an	að *t*ala, að *t*aka, ú*t*i (to talk, to take, outdoors)
U u (u)	like French *u* as in t*u*	h*u*nd*u*r, að m*u*na, *u*ndir (dog, to remember, under)
Ú ú (ú)	y*ou*	þ*ú*, *ú*ti, *ú*lpa (you, outdoors, winter jacket)
V v (vaff)	*v*ine	að *v*elja, *v*ín, *v*ondur (to choose, wine, bad)
X x (ex)	fa*x*	se*x*, ke*x*, va*x* (six, crackers, wax)
Y y (yfsilon y)	t*i*n (same sound as the Icelandic letter **i**)	þ*y*rstur, að k*y*nnast (thirsty, to get to know somebody)
Ý ý (yfsilon ý)	s*ee* (same sound as the Icelandic letter **í**)	n*ý*r, *ý*mis, k*ý*r (new, various, cow)

Þ þ (þorn)	*th*istle (always word- or syllable-initial)	**það, íþróttir, að þekkja** (it, sports, to know)
Æ æ (æ)	d*i*ne	**fæ, æfing, að ætla** (get, exercise, to intend)
Ö ö (ö)	like the vowel sound preceding *r* in *girl* and *worker*	**gömul, öld, gjöf** (old, century, gift)

It is important to memorize the Icelandic letter order, especially when using a dictionary.

Special Letter Combinations

The letter combinations **au**, **ei**, and **ey** are pronounced in a special way in Icelandic:

au	Start with an Icelandic **ö** sound then make an *ee* sound (as in *see*)	**þau, sundlaug, að kaupa** (they, swimming pool, to buy)
ei	d*ay*	**leiður, eins, deild** (sad, alike, department)
ey	d*ay*	**leyfi, eyja, peysa** (permission, island, sweater)

Pronunciation of vowels before *ng* and *nk*

Vowels before **ng** and **nk** go through a change and are pronounced differently than usual. A summary of the vowel changes is shown below:

Example	Pronunciation due to ng/nk rule
banki bank	*ou* as in l*ou*d
fingur finger	*ee* as in s*ee*
lunga lung	*ou* as in y*ou*
engill angel	*ei* as in d*ay*
löng long	*au*- start with an Icelandic **ö** sound then make an *ee* sound (as in *see*)
syngur sings	*ee* as in s*ee*

Double Consonants

Double consonants such as **mm**, **bb**, and **rr** are pronounced as longer sounds than their single-consonant counterparts. The sounds **p**, **t**, and **k** are pronounced with a breath of air before them when these consonants are doubled. Thus, **pp** is pronounced close to *hp*, **tt** is pronounced *ht*, and **kk** is pronounced *hk*.

Word	Pronunciation
að stoppa to stop	*að stohpa*
hattur hat	*hahtur*
sokkur sock	*sohkur*

There are two double consonants that have a special pronunciation: **ll** and **nn**.

Double-l is pronounced with a *t*-insertion, so that it becomes **tl**. The word **sæll** *hi* is pronounced more like *sætl*. You should practice this quite a lot since it occurs often in Icelandic. Note that the *t*-insertion does not occur in loan words such as **grilla** *to barbecue* and nicknames such as **Halli** or **Kalli** (short for Haraldur and Karl).

Word	Pronunciation
bíll car	*bítl*
Páll Paul	*Pátl*

The following are a few examples of words with **double-l** that do not have a *t*-insertion:

grilla	barbecue	**Halli**	Halli
ball	dance ball	**Kalli**	Kalli

Double-n is also pronounced with a *t*-insertion, but only after an accented vowel or the special letter combinations **au**, **ei**, and **ey**. The word **einn** *one* is pronounced *eitn* because the **double-n** follows the letter combination **ei**, and the word **fínn** *elegant* is pronounced *fítn* because the accent is on the vowel preceding the **double-n**. The verb **að finna** *to find*, however, does not have *t*-insertion in it since the **i** before the **double-n** is not accented.

Word	Pronunciation
ei**nn** one	*eitn*
fí**nn** elegant	*fítn*
hrei**nn** clean	*hreitn*

The following words are pronounced without *t*-insertion:

að finna	to find
minn	my

T-insertion occurs in other Icelandic consonant combinations that are not double consonants but are worth bringing up here. The consonant clusters **sl**, **sn**, **rl**, and **rn** are pronounced respectively *stl, stn, rtl,* and *rtn*.

Word	Pronunciation
ru**sl** trash	*rustl*
a**sn**i donkey	*astni*
ka**rl** man	*kartl*
ho**rn** horn	*hortn*

Stress

By stress, we generally mean which syllables receive most of the emphasis when speaking. Compare in English: "I sub<u>je</u>ct myself to hard work" with "My s<u>u</u>bject is the future of robots." Notice that in the first sentence, "subject" receives stress on the second syllable while in the second sentence the stress is on the first syllable.

In Icelandic, the stress pattern does not change word to word. Stress in Icelandic is always on the first syllable. Secondary stress or half-stress sometimes occurs in longer words, but the important thing to remember is that the first syllable of a word must be stressed. This is especially important for words which are similar in Icelandic and English since it is very tempting to pronounce them as they are pronounced in English. Compare where the stress is in Icelandic versus English:

English Stress	Icelandic stress
banana	banani
America	Ameríka
October	október
Italian	ítalskur
Atlantic Ocean	Atlantshaf

Length of Vowels

Vowels in Icelandic can be either short or long. If a syllable is unstressed, its vowel is always short; if a syllable is stressed, its vowel is long. However, if a stressed syllable occurs before a double consonant, its vowel is short. Thus, in **dama** *lady*, the first **a** is long and the second is short. However, in **amma** *grandmother*, the first **a** is short and so is the second **a**.

Also, a vowel is long if it is followed by **pr**, **tr**, **kr**, **gr**, or **gð**.

akrar fields   **bragð** taste   **apríl** April

A vowel is short before **pn**, **tn**, **kn**, **pl**, **tl**, or **kl**.

að sakna to miss   **epli** apple
að opna to open   **setning** sentence

How to use this book

This book is designed to provide the reader with a general vocabulary of common words and the basics of Icelandic grammar. The material it covers is equivalent to a first-year university course in Icelandic. Each lesson introduces everyday situations in which visitors to Iceland could find themselves. Upon completing the book, readers will have the vocabulary and grammar that will enable them to participate in simple conversations on everyday topics.

The aim of this book is to present the basic grammatical structure of Icelandic. The most common categories of regular nouns and the conjugation of verbs in the present tense will be introduced. For ease of use, the grammatical discussion has been simplified and exceptions are generally not noted. The past tense of verbs and the subjunctive form are not addressed, although a few instances of these forms occur in the dialogues.

LESSON 1

Kveðjur

◇◇◇◇◇◇

Greetings

Samtal 1: Kveðjur

Jeremy situr á kaffistofu háskólans og er að drekka kaffi. Kona sem situr við borðið fer að tala við hann.

Hrafnhildur:	Sæll.
Jeremy:	Sæl.
Hrafnhildur:	Ég heiti Hrafnhildur. Hvað heitir þú?
Jeremy:	Ég heiti Jeremy.
Hrafnhildur:	Ertu nemandi hér?
Jeremy:	Já, ég er að læra íslensku.
Hrafnhildur:	En frábært! Hvaðan ertu?
Jeremy:	Ég er frá Bandaríkjunum. Hvað ert þú að læra?
Hrafnhildur:	Ég er ekki nemandi. Ég kenni sagnfræði.
Jeremy:	Ertu kennari?
Hrafnhildur:	Já, ég er kennari.
Jeremy:	Jæja, tíminn er að byrja. Ég verð að fara.
Hrafnhildur:	Já, ég líka. Við sjáumst kannski seinna.
Jeremy:	Já, það var gaman að kynnast þér.
Hrafnhildur:	Sömuleiðis. Við sjáumst!
Jeremy:	Bless bless!

Samtal 2

Næsta dag hittir Jeremy Hrafnhildi og manninn hennar Gunnar á kaffistofunni.

Hrafnhildur:	Hæ Jeremy!
Jeremy:	Nei, blessuð! Gaman að sjá þig!
Hrafnhildur:	Sömuleiðis. Hvað segirðu gott?
Jeremy:	Allt gott bara. En þú?
Hrafnhildur:	Allt þetta fína. Hvernig gengur námið?
Jeremy:	Það gengur bara vel.
Hrafnhildur:	Þetta er maðurinn minn.

Dialogue 1: Greetings

Jeremy is sitting in the university cafeteria having a cup of coffee. A woman sitting at his table starts talking to him.

Hrafnhildur:	Hello.
Jeremy:	Hello.
Hrafnhildur:	My name is Hrafnhildur. What is your name?
Jeremy:	My name is Jeremy.
Hrafnhildur:	Are you a student here?
Jeremy:	Yes, I am learning Icelandic.
Hrafnhildur:	Oh great! Where are you from?
Jeremy:	I am from the United States. What are you studying?
Hrafnhildur:	I am not a student. I teach history.
Jeremy:	Are you a teacher?
Hrafnhildur:	Yes, I am a teacher.
Jeremy:	Oh, the class is starting. I have to go.
Hrafnhildur:	Yes, me too. We'll see each other later maybe.
Jeremy:	Yes, it was nice to meet you.
Hrafnhildur:	Likewise. See you!
Jeremy:	Bye, bye!

Dialogue 2

The following day, Jeremy meets Hrafnhildur and her husband Gunnar in the cafeteria.

Hrafnhildur:	Hi, Jeremy!
Jeremy:	Hello! Great to see you!
Hrafnhildur:	Likewise. How are you?
Jeremy:	Alright. And you?
Hrafnhildur:	Alright. How are your studies going?
Jeremy:	It's going well.
Hrafnhildur:	This is my husband.

Gunnar:	Komdu sæll, ég heiti Gunnar.
Jeremy:	Blessaður, ég heiti Jeremy.
Hrafnhildur:	Jeremy er frá Bandaríkjunum. Hann er að læra íslensku.
Gunnar:	En gaman!
Jeremy:	Ert þú líka kennari?
Gunnar:	Nei, ég er leikari.
Jeremy:	Þetta er Jennifer. Hún er líka að læra íslensku.
Gunnar og Hrafnhildur:	Komdu sæl!
Jennifer:	Sæl og blessuð!

Gunnar:	Hello, my name is Gunnar.
Jeremy:	Hello, my name is Jeremy.
Hrafnhildur:	Jeremy is from the United States. He is studying Icelandic.
Gunnar:	Oh great!
Jeremy:	Are you also a teacher?
Gunnar:	No, I am an actor.
Jeremy:	This is Jennifer. She is also studying Icelandic.
Gunnar and Hrafnhildur:	Hello!
Jennifer:	Hello!

How to use the vocabulary lists in this book

Some of the words in the vocabulary lists in this book appear in a form that is slightly different from that which you see in the dialogues. This is because of rules of grammar that you will learn later, but as an introduction, here are some basic rules which explain these differences.

1. *Nouns,* *adjectives,* and *pronouns* have four different cases: nominative, accusative, dative, and genitive. These cases also exist in singular and plural. The use of cases is explained in Lessons 9–14. The vocabulary lists show the basic form, which is the nominative singular.

2. *Nouns* can be either definite or indefinite. Icelandic does not have an indefinite article (a, an), and the definite article is added to the end of a noun as a suffix. In the vocabulary list, nouns are listed without the definite article.

3. *Adjectives* exist in three different genders: masculine, feminine, and neuter. The adjectives in the vocabulary lists will appear in the same gender as they appear in the text. However, in the glossary at the back of this book, all adjectives are given in the masculine nominative case since that is the form that is shown in dictionaries. Gender of adjectives is addressed in Lesson 4.

4. Regular *verbs* in the present tense follow five different patterns which are referred to as categories *v1–v5*. The verb categories will be noted in the vocabulary lists. See Lesson 6 for details.

Orðaforði – Vocabulary

að *infinitive marker* to
allt *pron.* everything
Bandaríkin *n. neu. pl. def.* United States
bara *adv.* only, just
bless *interj.* bye
blessaður *adj. m.* hi! *(to a man)*
blessuð *adj. f.* hi! *(to a woman)*
að byrja *v1* to start
ekki *adv.* not, don't
en *conj.* but
ég *pron.* I
að fara *v4* **(ég fer)** to go
fína *see* **fínn**

fínn *adj. m.* fine
frá *prep.* from
frábært *adj. neu.* great
gaman *n. neu.* fun
að ganga *v3* **(ég geng)** walk, go (I walk)
gengur *v3 (3ʳᵈ pers. sing., see* **að ganga***)*
 he walks
gott *adj. neu.* good
að heita *v2* to be called
hér *adv.* here
hvað *pron.* what
hvaðan *adv.* where … from
hvernig *pron.* how

íslenska *n. f.* Icelandic
já *interj.* yes
jæja *interj.* well! okay!
kannski *adv.* maybe
að kenna *v2* to teach
kennari *n. m.* teacher
kynnast *v2 st-form* to get to know, to meet
leikari *n. m.* actor
líka *adv.* also
að læra *v2* to study, to learn
nám *n. neu.* studies, learning
nemandi *n. m.* student
sagnfræði *n. f.* history
segirðu *v2 (2ⁿᵈ pers. sing., see **að segja**)* you say
að segja *v2* to say

seinna *adv.* later
að sjá *v5* **(ég sé)** to see
sjáumst *v5 st-form* see you!
sæll *adj. m.* hi! *(to a man)*
sæl *adj. f.* hi! *(to a woman)*
sömuleiðis *adv.* likewise
tími *n. m.* class, time
var *v. irr., past, see **að vera** was
vel *adv.* well, good
að vera *v. irr.* to be
að verða *v3* to become
við *pron.* we
það *pron.* it
þetta *pron.* this
þig *pron. acc.* you *(sing.)*
þú *pron.* you *(sing.)*
þér *pron. dat.* you *(sing.)*

Orðasambönd – Useful expressions

Hvað segirðu gott?	How are you doing?
Hvað er að frétta?	What's up?
Allt gott *(bara).*	Just fine.
Allt ágætt *(bara).*	Just fine.
Allt þetta fína.	Everything is just great.
Ekkert sérstakt.	Nothing special. *(i.e. neither good nor bad)*
Fyrirgefðu.	Sorry.
Fyrirgefiði.	Sorry. *(to more than one person)*
Afsakaðu.	Excuse me.
Afsakið.	Excuse me. *(to more than one person)*
Takk.	Thanks.
Þakka þér fyrir.	Thank you.
Þakka ykkur fyrir.	Thank you. *(to more than one person)*
Allt í lagi.	Okay, no problem.
Ekkert mál!	No problem!
Ég heiti ...	My name is ... *(for first names)*
Ég er kallaður ...	I'm called ... *(for nicknames, men)*
Ég er kölluð ...	I'm called ... *(for nicknames, women)*
Þetta er ...	This is ...

How to greet someone

Greetings in formal and informal encounters

The traditional Icelandic greetings are the words **sæll** (*lit.: happy*) and **blessaður** (*lit.: blessed*). When you use a greeting, you have to consider the gender and the number of the person or people you are greeting:

Greetings

To a man	To a woman or to a mixed group	To more than one man	To more than one woman
sæll	sæl	sælir	sælar
blessaður	blessuð	blessaðir	blessaðar
blessaður og sæll	blessuð og sæl	blessaðir og sælir	blessaðar og sælar

You can also add the imperative **komdu** *(sing.)* or **komiði** *(pl.) come* in front of the greetings above: **komdu sæl, komdu sæll og blessaður**.

To family members, close friends, and people you meet every day: Many Icelanders, especially young people, use the more colloquial greeting **hæ** which is equivalent to *hi*.

Greetings in formal situations and in service encounters

From dawn until around six o'clock:

Góðan dag   Good day
Góðan daginn

The phrases **góðan dag** and **góðan daginn** are also used in informal encounters in the same way that you would use the phrase *good morning* in English. For example, you could use **góðan dag** when you sit down at the breakfast table.

Note that there is no phrase that translates literally as *good morning* in Icelandic.

From six o'clock until late night:

Gott kvöld   Good evening
Góða kvöldið

Goodbyes

For saying goodbye the following phrases can be used:

Bless!	Bye!
Bless bless!	Bye bye!
Sjáumst!	See you!
Heyrumst!	I will hear from you!
Blessaður!	Goodbye! *(to a man)*
Blessuð!	Goodbye! *(to a woman)*
Vertu sæll!	Goodbye! *(to a man)*
Vertu sæl!	Goodbye! *(to a woman)*
Bæ!	Bye! *(very informal)*

The phrase **góða nótt** *good night* is only used when someone is going to sleep or when you are saying goodbye to someone very late in the evening.

Personal pronouns

Learn the pronouns by heart:

Personal Pronouns

Person	Singular		Plural	
1ˢᵗ	**ég**	I	**við**	we
2ⁿᵈ	**þú**	you	**þið**	you
3ʳᵈ *m.* *f.* *neu.*	**hann** **hún** **það**	he she it	**þeir** **þær** **þau**	they

Remember that there are three different pronouns for third person plural. When you refer to more than one woman you use the pronoun **þær**; when you refer to more than one man you use the pronoun **þeir**; and when you refer to a mixed group you use the pronoun **þau**.

Jóhann og Óli = **þeir**	Jeremy and John = **þeir**
Guðrún og Hrafnhildur = **þær**	Jennifer and Mary = **þær**
Hrafnhildur og Óli = **þau**	Jeremy and Jennifer = **þau**

Verb conjugation and the verb *að heita* (to be called)

When you construct a sentence, you need to conjugate verbs by adding inflectional endings to their stems. The inflectional endings are governed by both person and number. The verb **heita** conjugates as follows (the stem is **heit**):

að heit-a (to be called)

Person	Singular			Plural		
1st	ég	heit-*i*	I am called	við	heit-*um*	we are called
2nd	þú	heit-*ir*	you are called	þið	heit-*ið*	you are called
3rd *m.*	hann		he	þeir		
f.	hún	heit-*ir*	she is called	þær	heit-*a*	they are called
neu.	það		it	þau		

Verbs that conjugate with the same endings as **að heit-a** are Category 2 verbs and are marked in the vocabulary lists and glossaries as *v2*. (We will return to the various categories of verbs in Chapter 6.)

Æfingar – Exercises

1. **Choose the right greeting.**

   a. You meet your best friend on the street *(a man)*:
   _____

   b. You are working in a bank and a customer comes in:
   _____

   c. You are going for a walk in the evening and you meet people you don't know:
   _____

   d. You are sitting in your kitchen and your eight-year-old sister comes home from school:
   _____

   e. You are meeting your girlfriends in a café:
   _____

f.   You are visiting your grandparents:

_____

g.   You are watching TV late in the evening and your brother gets
     up and says he is going to bed:

_____

2. **Translate the following sentences into Icelandic. Pay special
    attention to the verb conjugation.**

a.   My name is Hrafnhildur.

_____

b.   Her name is Anna.

_____

c.   His name is Óli.

_____

d.   Their names are Anna and Óli.

_____

e.   Our names are Hrafnhildur and Óli.

_____

f.   Their names are Anna and Hrafnhildur.

_____

3. **Choose the right pronoun.**

a.   Óli og Jóhann_____
b.   Hrafnhildur_____
c.   Óli_____
d.   Ég og þú_____
e.   Þú og hún_____
f.   Anna og Óli_____

4. **Translate the following conversation. You may have to use the list of useful expressions found in this chapter.**

In a bank:
A: Good morning!

_____

B: Good morning!

_____

A: What is your name?

_____

B: My name is Anna Jónsdóttir.

_____

A: Is your name Anna Ómarsdóttir?

_____

B: No, Anna Jónsdóttir.

_____

A: Sorry.

_____

B: No problem.

_____

LESSON 2

Talarðu íslensku?

◇◇◇◇◇◇

Do you speak Icelandic?

Samtal: Talarðu íslensku?

Hrafnhildur og Jeremy eru að tala saman í háskólanum.

Óli:	Hæ Hrafnhildur! Hvað segirðu gott?
Hrafnhildur:	Blessaður, allt þetta fína. En þú?
Óli:	Allt gott bara.
Hrafnhildur:	Óli, þetta er Jeremy. Hann er frá Bandaríkjunum.
Óli:	Hello, nice to meet you!
Jeremy:	Sæll. Já, sömuleiðis, gaman að kynnast þér.
Óli:	Ha? Talarðu íslensku?
Jeremy:	Já, ég tala smá íslensku.
Óli:	Hvað ertu að segja? En frábært!
Jeremy:	Ég er að læra íslensku.
Óli:	Og hvernig gengur það?
Jeremy:	Það gengur bara vel. En hvað gerir þú?
Óli:	Ég er að læra frönsku.
Jeremy:	En gaman! Við getum þá talað saman á frönsku!
Óli:	Nei, ekki enn. Ég er að læra frönsku! Ég tala ekki svo vel.

Dialogue: Do you speak Icelandic?

Hrafnhildur and Jeremy are talking at the University.

Óli:	Hello Hrafnhildur! How are you?
Hrafnhildur:	Hello, I'm fine. And you?
Óli:	I'm okay.
Hrafnhildur:	Óli, this is Jeremy. He is from the United States.
Óli:	Hello, nice to meet you!
Jeremy:	Hello. Yes, likewise it's great to meet you.
Óli:	Huh? Do you speak Icelandic?
Jeremy:	Yes, I speak a bit.
Óli:	Really? That's great!
Jeremy:	I am studying Icelandic.
Óli:	And how is that going?
Jeremy:	It's going well. And what do you do?
Óli:	I'm studying French.
Jeremy:	Oh great! We could speak together in French then!
Óli:	No, not yet. I am just learning French! I don't speak so well.

Orðaforði – Vocabulary

enn *adv.* still
franska *n. f.* French, referring to the language
að gera *v2* to do
háskóli *n. m.* university
hvernig *pron.* how

saman *adv.* together
að segja *v2* to say
smá *adv.* a bit
svo *adv.* so
að tala *v1* to speak, to talk

Orðasambönd – Useful expressions

Hvað ertu að segja!	Really! *(response to something that seems unbelievable)*
Ha?	What did you say? *(informal)*
Ha, hvað segirðu?	Huh, what did you say? *(informal)*
Hvað segirðu?	What did you say?
Fyrirgefðu, hvað segirðu?	Excuse me, what did you say?
Fyrirgefðu, ég skil þig ekki.	Sorry, I don't understand you.
Geturðu talað *(aðeins)* hægar?	Can you speak *(a bit)* slower?
Þú talar of hratt fyrir mig.	You speak too quickly for me.
Geturðu útskýrt þetta aftur?	Could you explain this again?
En frábært!	That's great!
En skemmtilegt!	That's fun!
En leiðinlegt!	That's bad!

The verb *að vera* (to be)

The verb **að vera** *to be* is an irregular verb. Learn the conjugation by heart:

að vera (to be)

Person	Singular			Plural		
1st	ég	er	I am	við	er-*um*	we are
2nd	þú	er-*t*	you are	þið	er-*uð*	you are
3rd *m.*	hann		he	þeir		
f.	hún	er	she is	þær	er-*u*	they are
neu.	það		it	þau		

Jeremy *er* frá Bandaríkjunum.
Jeremy is from the United States.

Hrafnhildur og Gunnar *eru* ekki frá Bandaríkjunum.
Hrafnhildur and Gunnar are not from the United States.

Regular verb: *að tala* (to talk, to speak)

The verb **að tala** *to talk, to speak* is a regular verb:

að tal-a (to talk, to speak)

Person	Singular			Plural		
1ˢᵗ	ég	tal-*a*	I speak	við	töl-*um*	we speak
2ⁿᵈ	þú	tal-*ar*	you speak	þið	tal-*ið*	you speak
3ʳᵈ m. f. neu.	hann hún það	tal-*ar*	he she speaks it	þeir þær þau	tal-*a*	they speak

Notice that the **a** sound shifts to an **ö** in the first person plural (**við tölum**). This shift takes place because of the **u** sound in the inflectional ending.

Ég tal*a* of mikið.	I talk too much.
Þú tal*ar* alltof mikið!	You talk way too much!

Hrafnhildur og Jeremy
    tal*a* íslensku.
	Hrafnhildur and Jeremy
	    speak Icelandic.

Verbs that conjugate with the same endings as **að tala** are Category 1 verbs and are marked in the vocabulary lists and glossaries as *v1*. (We will return to the various categories of verbs in Chapter 6.)

Progressive with the verb *að vera* (to be)

The verb **að vera** *to be* is often used in verb combinations. This construction has a similar meaning to the progressive continuous in English: *she is studying.* The first verb in the combination is subject to conjugation (see conjugation above), while the main verb is always in the infinitive (the basic form), preceded by the infinitive marker **að** *to.*

Hrafnhildur *er að* tala.	Hrafnhildur *is speaking.*
Jeremy *er að* læra íslensku.	Jeremy *is learning* Icelandic.

Ég skil ekki hvað þú *ert*
    ***að* segja.**
	I don't understand what you
	    are saying.

The *st*-form of the verb

The greetings **sjáumst** *see you* and **heyrumst** *I will hear from you* are both examples of the **st**-form of verbs. The **st**-forms typically have a reflexive or a reciprocal meaning. A verb is reflexive when the subject of the sentence is doing something to itself, such as in *she hurt herself*. It is reciprocal when two subjects are doing something to each other, such as in *they greeted each other*. In the case of **sjáumst**, the literal translation is *we will see each other*, and the literal translation of **heyrumst** is *we will hear each other*.

Phonetically reduced *þú* (you) in yes/no questions

When you create a yes/no question, the pronoun **þú** *you* is dropped and **ðu, tu**, or **u** are added to the end of the verb. The endings are phonetically reduced versions of **þú** *you*. Note also that the vowel changes from the **ú** to **u**.

Verbs that end in an **r** add **ðu**:

Talar þú íslensku? → **Talar*ðu* íslensku?**
Do you speak Icelandic?

When the inflectional ending in second person singular ends with **t** or **ð**, such as is the case for the verb **að vera** (**þú ert**/*you are*), the verb only adds **u**.

Ert þú að tala íslensku? → **Ert*u* að tala íslensku?**
Are you speaking Icelandic?

Æfingar – Exercises

1. **Fill in the blanks with the correct form of the verb *að vera* (to be).**

    a. Þetta _____ ég.
    b. Mamma _____ ekki hér.
    c. Við _____ að lesa.
    d. Þú _____ mjög skemmtileg(ur)!
    e. Hver _____ þú?
    f. Hver _____ þetta?
    g. Við _____ frá Íslandi.
    h. Þið _____ í háskóla.

2. Fill in the blanks with the correct form of the verb *að tala* (to speak).

a. Ég _____ frönsku og ensku.

b. Hvað _____ þú?

c. Þeir _____ ekki íslensku.

d. Þau _____ ensku.

e. Við _____ saman á íslensku.

3. Translate the following sentences.

a. This is John. He is studying French.

_____

b. Hrafnhildur is speaking Icelandic.

_____

c. You *(pl.)* are studying Icelandic.

_____

d. Do you speak French?

_____

LESSON 3

Morgunmatur

◇◇◇◇◇◇

Breakfast

Samtal: Morgunmatur

Hrafnhildur og Gunnar eru búin að bjóða Jeremy í morgunmat.

Hrafnhildur:	Fáðu þér sæti, Jeremy.
Gunnar:	Hér er diskur og hnífur handa þér.
Jeremy:	Takk.
Hrafnhildur:	Vantar ekki glas?
Gunnar:	Jú, það vantar glas. Jeremy, má bjóða þér kaffi eða te?

Jeremy:	Kaffi takk.
Gunnar:	Viltu mjólk eða sykur?
Jeremy:	Nei takk, bara svart og sykurlaust.
Gunnar:	Gjörðu svo vel.
Hrafnhildur:	Hér er svo appelsínusafi ef þú vilt.
Jeremy:	Takk.
Gunnar:	Og svo er hér brauð, smjör og álegg. Hér er til dæmis íslenskur ostur og hangikjöt.

Jeremy:	Hangikjöt? Hvað er það?
Hrafnhildur:	Hangikjöt er reykt lambakjöt.
Gunnar:	Það er mjög gott! Smakkaðu!
Jeremy:	Mmm. Já, þetta er mjög gott. Þetta er líka alveg rosalega gott brauð.
Hrafnhildur:	Já, ég fór í bakarí í morgun. Það er alveg nýtt.

Jeremy:	En hvað er þetta?
Hrafnhildur:	Þetta er skyr.
Jeremy:	Hvað er skyr?
Hrafnhildur:	Skyr er líka séríslenskur réttur. Það er kannski svipað og jógúrt.
Gunnar:	Já, þú verður að smakka skyr. Það er líka mjög gott.
Jeremy:	Mmm. Já, þetta er bara ágætt.
Hrafnhildur:	Fáðu þér meira!
Jeremy:	Nei takk. Ég er orðinn saddur.
Gunnar:	En viltu ekki smá ábót á kaffið?
Jeremy:	Jú takk. Kannski tíu dropa.

Dialogue: Breakfast

Hrafnhildur and Gunnar have invited Jeremy for breakfast.

Hrafnhildur:	Have a seat, Jeremy.
Gunnar:	Here is a plate and a knife for you.
Jeremy:	Thank you.
Hrafnhildur:	Is there a glass missing?
Gunnar:	Yes, there is a glass missing. Jeremy, may I offer you coffee or tea?
Jeremy:	Coffee please.
Gunnar:	Do you want milk or sugar?
Jeremy:	No, thank you, just black without sugar.
Gunnar:	Here you go.
Hrafnhildur:	Here is some orange juice if you'd like.
Jeremy:	Thank you.
Gunnar:	And here are bread, butter, and some things to put on the bread. For example there is Icelandic cheese and **hangikjöt**.
Jeremy:	**Hangikjöt**? What is that?
Hrafnhildur:	**Hangikjöt** is smoked lamb.
Gunnar:	It's really good. Try some!
Jeremy:	Mmm. Yes, it's really good. This is also really good bread.
Hrafnhildur:	Yes, I went to the bakery this morning. The bread is completely fresh.
Jeremy:	But what is that?
Hrafnhildur:	That's **skyr**.
Jeremy:	What is **skyr**?
Hrafnhildur:	**Skyr** is also an especially Icelandic food. It is a bit like yogurt.
Gunnar:	Yes, you have to try **skyr**. It's also very good.
Jeremy:	Mmm. Yes, this is quite good.
Hrafnhildur:	Have some more!
Jeremy:	No, thank you. I am full.
Gunnar:	But do you want some more coffee?
Jeremy:	Yes, thank you. Just a bit.

Orðaforði – Vocabulary

alveg *adv.* totally
appelsínusafi *n. m.* orange juice
ábót *n. f.* seconds, a second helping
ágætt *adj. neu.* fine
álegg *n. neu.* things to put on bread
að bjóða *v3* (**ég býð**) to invite, to offer
    (I invite)
brauð *n. neu.* bread
diskur *n. m.* plate
dropi *n. m.* drop
ef *conj.* if
að fara *v4* (**ég fer**) to go
fáðu *v. imp.* have!
fór *v4 (past, see* **að fara***)* went
glas *n. neu.* glass
hangikjöt *n. neu.* smoked lamb
    (Icelandic specialty)
hnífur *n. m.* knife
jógúrt *n. neu. or f.* yogurt
jú *interj.* yes
kaffi *n. neu.* coffee
lambakjöt *n. neu.* lamb *(meat)*
meira *adv. or adj.* more
mjólk *n. f.* milk
mjög *adv.* very

morgunmatur *n. m.* breakfast
nýtt *adj. neu.* new
orðinn (*see* **að verða**)
ostur *n. m.* cheese
reykt *adj. neu.* smoked
réttur *n. m.* dish
rosalega *adv.* very
saddur *adj. m.* full
séríslenskur *adj. m.* especially Icelandic
skyr *n. neu. skyr,* a yogurt-like specialty
að smakka *v1* to taste
smakkaðu *v1 imp.* taste!
smjör *n. neu.* butter
sykur *n. m.* sugar
sykurlaust *adj. neu.* sugar-free
svart *adj. neu.* black
svipað *adj. neu.* similar
sæti *n. neu.* seat
takk *interj.* thanks
te *n. neu.* tea
tíu *num.* ten
að vanta *v1* to lack, to need
að vilja *v. irr.* to want
að verða *v3* to become, to have to

Orðasambönd – Useful expressions

Er til meira …
    skyr?
    kaffi?
    te?
    brauð?

Do you have more …
    skyr *(Icelandic yogurt-like specialty)*?
    coffee?
    tea?
    bread?

Má bjóða þér meira …
    kaffi?
    te?

Can I offer you more …
    coffee?
    tea?

Já takk.
Já, endilega!
Já, kannski tíu dropa.

Yes please.
Yes, sure!
Yes, maybe a little bit. *(Only said about coffee.)*

Nei takk.	No thanks.
Nei takk, ég er mjög södd.	No thanks, I'm very full *(f.)*.
Nei takk, ég er mjög saddur.	No thanks, I'm very full *(m.)*.
Þetta er rosalega gott!	This is very good!
Mmm hvað þetta er gott!	Mmm this is very good!
Þetta er alveg ágætt.	This is quite good.

Gender of nouns

Icelandic has three genders: masculine (**hann** *he*), feminine (**hún** *she*) and neuter (**það** *it*). Each noun has only one gender, and the gender never changes. The noun **ostur** *cheese*, for example, is always masculine. It is very important to know the gender of nouns, as the different genders have different inflectional endings, such as the plural ending, definite articles, and case inflections, all of which we will learn later.

Gender is a grammatical category. That means that the gender of nouns does not have anything to do with the natural gender of the people, objects, or ideas to which it refers. In fact, the grammatical and natural gender may in some cases seem to contradict each other, for example, when a feminine noun refers to a man and vice versa. Thus, the noun **kvenmaður** *woman* is a masculine word although it refers to a woman. The noun **karlmennska** *masculinity*, on the other hand, is a feminine word.

In the same way, it may seem strange at first to refer to inanimate objects by the pronouns **hann** *he* and **hún** *she*. In Icelandic, the noun **sími** *telephone* is a masculine noun. Therefore, we refer to it by using the pronoun **hann** *he*.

It is important also to note that in the case of compound words, the gender is determined by the last word in the compound. The word **súkkulaðikaka** *chocolate cake* is thus feminine since **kaka** *cake* is a feminine noun.

There are no unfailing rules that can be used to find the right gender of nouns, but the following chart can help guide you. It shows the typical endings for nouns in nominative singular. Nominative singular is the basic form of nouns. Remember that other cases have other endings (see Lessons 9–14).

Masculine endings	Feminine endings	Neuter endings
ur	–	$–^2$
r	a	a^3
ll	ing^1	i^4
nn		
i		

1. Note that *ing* is not an ending but a suffix which occurs in other genders as well. However, only feminine nouns end in *ing* in nominative.
2. Nouns with no ending and an *a* in the stem are usually neuter.
3. Many words in this category refer to parts of the body.
4. Note that the final *i* is not an ending but a part of the stem.

Unfortunately, there are many exceptions to these rules. Therefore, you will need to memorize the gender for some of the words in this beginner's course. Try to memorize the gender for each noun when you learn it. The vocabulary lists included in each lesson will show which gender each noun belongs to *(m. = masculine, f. = feminine, neu. = neuter)*.

Masculine Nouns

ur	**maður** man	**diskur** disc, CD, plate	**ostur** cheese	
r	**skór** shoe	**sjór** ocean	**bær** town, farm	
ll	**stóll** chair	**bíll** car	**lykill** key	
nn	**steinn** stone	**sveinn** boy		
i	**kennari** teacher	**pabbi** dad	**afi** grandfather	**safi** juice

Feminine Nouns

–	**borg** city	**mynd** picture	**búð** store
a	**mamma** mom	**klukka** clock	**kærasta** girlfriend
ing	**spurning** question	**æfing** exercise	

Neuter Nouns

–	**kjöt** meat **brauð** bread	**skyr** skyr	**barn** child	**land** country, land
a	**auga** eye **eyra** ear	**hjarta** heart	**pasta** pasta	**Kanada** Canada
i	**súkkulaði** chocolate	**kaffi** coffee	**veski** wallet	

Gender of adjectives

As mentioned above, each noun has one gender, and the gender does not change. Adjectives, on the other hand, always exist in all three genders. An adjective such as *Icelandic* is thus **íslenskur** when it refers to a masculine noun, **íslensk** when it refers to a feminine noun, and **íslenskt** when it refers to a neuter noun. The chart below shows three adjectives declined to match three different nouns.

Masculine Adj.	Feminine Adj.	Neuter Adj.
ur	–	t
íslensk*ur* ost*ur*	íslensk mjólk	íslensk*t* skyr
Icelandic cheese	Icelandic milk	Icelandic skyr

The grammatical gender of the noun **kennari** *teacher* is masculine. Therefore, even though Hrafnhildur is a woman, the adjective modifying **kennari** *teacher* has a masculine ending.

Hrafnhildur er skemmtileg.	Hrafnhildur is fun.
Hrafnhildur er skemmtileg*ur* kennari.	Hrafnhildur is a fun teacher.
Hrafnhildur er skemmtileg kona.	Hrafnhildur is a fun woman.

Answering questions yes: *já* vs. *jú*

Icelandic, like many other languages, has two ways of answering *yes* depending upon how a question is first posed. If the question is positively expressed, as in *Is there a glass missing?* the affirmative answer to it is then **já**. However, if the question is negatively expressed, as in *Is there not a glass missing?* the affirmative answer is then **jú**.

Vantar glas?	Is there a glass missing?
Já.	Yes.

Vantar ekki glas?	Isn't there a glass missing?
Jú.	Yes.

In both instances (**já** and **jú**), the translation in English would be *yes*.

Word order

The word order in Icelandic is similar to English (see Lesson 5 for an important exception, the verb-second rule).

Declarative Sentence

Subject	Verb	Adverbial	Object/Predicate
Ég	tala		íslensku.
I	speak		Icelandic.
Þetta	er		skyr.
This	is		skyr.
Þetta	er	ekki	íslenskur ostur.
This	is	not	Icelandic cheese.

Yes and No Questions (the verb and subject switch place)

Verb	Subject	Adverbial	Object/Predicate
Talar	þú		íslensku?
Speak	you		Icelandic?
Er	þetta		skyr?
Is	this		skyr?
Er	þetta	ekki	íslenskur ostur?
Is	this	not	Icelandic cheese?

Interrogative Questions

Interrogative	Verb	Subject	Adverbial
Hver	er	þetta	þarna?
Who	is	that	there?
Hvað	er	þetta?	
What	is	this?	

Æfingar – Exercises

1. Find the gender of the following nouns.

a. lampi (lamp) _____
b. klukka (clock) _____
c. tölva (computer) _____
d. trefill (scarf) _____
e. lunga (lung) _____
f. banani (banana) _____
g. borð (table) _____
h. prestur (priest) _____
i. bók (book) _____
j. kokkur (cook) _____
k. glas (glass) _____
l. rúm (bed) _____
m. pottur (pot) _____
n. bjór (beer) _____
o. rúta (bus) _____
p. hundur (dog) _____
q. köttur (cat) _____

2. Fill in the blanks below with the correct adjectives.

rómantískur (romantic)
a. Þetta er mjög _____ saga.
b. Einar er _____ maður.
c. Erla er mjög _____ kona.
d. Rómeó er mjög _____ veitingastaður.

skemmtilegur (fun)
e. Þetta er mjög _____ hundur.
f. Þetta er _____ kennari.
g. Ísland er _____ land.

bandarískur (American)
h. Jeremy er _____
i. Guðrún er ekki _____
j. Steinbeck var _____ rithöfundur.

3. **Place the following words in the correct order to make declarative sentences.**

a. heitir   Óli   hann   ekki

_____

b. matur   íslenskur   þetta   er

_____

c. fallegt   land   Ísland   er

_____

d. ekki   bakarí   þetta   er

_____

4. **Change the word order to make questions.**

a. Þetta ert þú.

_____?

b. Þetta er íslenskt skyr.

_____?

c. Þú heitir Einar.

_____?

d. Hangikjöt er reykt lambakjöt.

_____?

LESSON 4

Hver ert þú?

◇◇◇◇◇◇

Who are you?

Samtal 1: Hver ert þú?

Klukkan er tólf og það er hádegishlé í skólanum. Jeremy og Jennifer
eru að borða nesti þegar blaðamaður kemur til þeirra og vill taka
viðtal.

Blaðamaður: Hver ert þú?
Jeremy: Ég heiti Jeremy og ég er skiptinemi frá Bandaríkjunum.

Blaðamaður: Hvað ertu búinn að vera lengi á Íslandi?
Jeremy: Ég er búinn að vera hér í fimm mánuði.
Blaðamaður: Og hvernig líkar þér?
Jeremy: Mér líkar mjög vel hérna.
Blaðamaður: Hvar ertu fæddur?
Jeremy: Ég er fæddur og uppalinn í New York.
Blaðamaður: Hvernig er að búa í New York?
Jeremy: Bara frábært. New York er mjög stór borg og þar er
                     alltaf eitthvað að gerast.
Blaðamaður: Hvernig manneskja ertu?
Jeremy: Ég er bara venjulegur strákur, alltaf hress og kátur.
Blaðamaður: Ertu hamingjusamur?
Jeremy: Já, svo sannarlega!

Samtal 2

Blaðamaður: En hvað heitir þú?
Jennifer: Ég heiti Jennifer
Blaðamaður: Hvaðan ertu?
Jennifer: Ég er frá Englandi.
Blaðamaður: Ertu frá London?
Jennifer: Nei, ég er úr sveit.
Blaðamaður: Hvernig er að vera í Reykjavík?
Jennifer: Það er gaman. Reykjavík er lítil en falleg borg. Hér er
                     nóg um að vera.
Blaðamaður: Hvað ertu að læra?

Dialogue 1: Who are you?

It is twelve o'clock and lunch break at school. Jeremy and Jennifer are eating lunch when a newspaper reporter who would like to conduct an interview arrives.

Reporter: Who are you?

Jeremy: My name is Jeremy, and I am an exchange student from the United States.

Reporter: How long have you been in Iceland?

Jeremy: I have been here for five months.

Reporter: And how do you like it?

Jeremy: I like it quite a lot.

Reporter: So where were you born?

Jeremy: I was born and brought up in New York.

Reporter: How is it living in New York?

Jeremy: Just great. New York is a very large city, and there is always something happening.

Reporter: What kind of person are you?

Jeremy: I am a regular guy, always in good spirits and jolly.

Reporter: Are you happy?

Jeremy: Yes, truly!

Dialogue 2

Reporter: What is your name?

Jennifer: My name is Jennifer.

Reporter: Where are you from?

Jennifer: I come from England.

Reporter: Are you from London?

Jennifer: No, I'm from the country.

Reporter: How do you find it in Reykjavik?

Jennifer: It's great. Reykjavik is a small and beautiful city. There is a lot going on.

Reporter: What are you studying?

Jennifer: Ég er myndlistarmaður en ég er að læra íslensku.

Blaðamaður: Hvernig myndirðu lýsa þér?

Jennifer: Ég er jákvæð en samt alvörugefin. Stundum er ég pínu feimin.

Blaðamaður: Og hér er ein spurning að lokum, ertu hamingjusöm?

Jennifer: Já, ég er mjög ánægð með lífið! Það er alveg frábært að vera hérna.

Blaðamaður: Takk fyrir þetta. Gangi þér vel!

Jennifer: Takk fyrir!

Jennifer: I am an artist, but I am studying Icelandic.

Reporter: How would you describe yourself?

Jennifer: I am positive yet serious. Sometimes I'm a bit shy.

Reporter: This is the last question: are you happy?

Jennifer: Yes, I really enjoy life! It's just great to be here.

Reporter: Thank you so much. Good luck!

Jennifer: Thank you!

Orðaforði – Vocabulary

alvörugefin *adj. f.* serious
ánægð *adj. f.* happy, pleased
blaðamaður *n. m.* newspaper reporter
að borða *v1* to eat
borg *n. f.* city
að búa *v5* **(ég bý)** to live
ein *num. f.* one
eitthvað *pron. neu.* something
falleg *adj. f.* beautiful
feimin *adj. f.* shy
fimm *num.* five
fæddur *adj. m.* born
að gerast *v2 st-form* to happen, take
    place
hamingjusamur *adj. m.* happy
hamingjusöm *adj. f.* happy
hádegishlé *n. neu.* lunch break
hér *adv.* here
hress *adj. m.* lively, healthy, in good
    spirits
hvernig *adv.* how
jákvæð *adj. f.* positive
kátur *adj. m.* glad, happy
klukka *n. f.* clock
að koma *v3* **(ég kem)** to come
lengi *adv.* long
að líka *v1* to like

lítil *adj. f.* small
að lýsa *v2* to describe
manneskja *n. f.* person, human being
mánuður *n. m.* month
mér *pron. dat.* I *(me)*
myndirðu *v2* would you
myndlistarmaður *n. m.* artist *(visual)*
nesti *n. neu.* packed lunch
nóg *adv.* enough
pína *n. f.* a bit
pínu *n. f. acc. (see* **pína***)*
sannarlega *adv.* truly
skiptinemi *n. m.* exchange student
skóli *n. m.* school
spurning *n. f.* question
stór *adj. f.* big
stundum *adv.* sometimes
sveit *n. f.* rural area
svo *adv.* so
að taka *v3* **(ég tek)** to take
tólf *num.* twelve
uppalinn *adj. m.* raised
venjulegur *n. m.* ordinary, normal
viðtal *n. neu.* interview
þegar *conj. or adv.* when
þeirra *pron. (gen.)* they

Names of countries

Ísland Iceland
Bandaríkin United States
Danmörk Denmark
England England
Frakkland France
Færeyjar Faroe Islands
Grænland Greenland

Kanada Canada
Finnland Finland
Noregur Norway
Rússland Russia
Svíþjóð Sweden
Þýskaland Germany

Ég bý ...	I live ...
á Íslandi.	in Iceland.
í Bandaríkjunum.	in the United States.
í Danmörku.	in Denmark.
á Englandi.	in England.
í Frakklandi.	in France.
í Færeyjum.	in the Faroe Islands.
á Grænlandi.	in Greenland.
í Kanada.	in Canada.
í Finnlandi.	in Finland.
í Noregi.	in Norway.
í Rússlandi.	in Russia.
í Svíþjóð.	in Sweden.
í Þýskalandi.	in Germany.

Ég er frá ...	I am from ...
Íslandi.	Iceland.
Bandaríkjunum.	the United States.
etc.	etc.

Adjectives

In Lesson 3 you learned that every adjective has three different genders and that it is the noun that determines what gender to assign. All the adjectives you learned followed exactly the same pattern. Unfortunately, not all adjectives are so easy to decline, and in this lesson we are going to look at the declension in more detail. Adjectives follow five different patterns, and we will now look at each category one at a time. Keep in mind that many adjectival stems correspond to the feminine form and only the masculine and neuter are formed by adding an inflectional ending.

Category 1 Adjectives (same as in Lesson 3):

Adjectives in this category add **ur** in masculine and **t** in neuter:

Category 1 Adjective Endings

Masculine	Feminine	Neuter
ur	–	t

Category 1 Adjectives

Masculine	Feminine	Neuter	English
íslensk-*ur*	íslensk	íslensk-*t*	Icelandic
skemmtileg-*ur*	skemmtileg	skemmtileg-*t*	fun
rómantísk-*ur*	rómantísk	rómantísk-*t*	romantic
leiðinleg-*ur*	leiðinleg	leiðinleg-*t*	boring

The *u*-shift in feminine adjectives:

When an adjective has an **a** sound in the stem such as in **svangur** *hungry*, that sound goes through a vowel shift and changes to **ö** in the feminine form of the adjective:

Masculine	Feminine	Neuter	English
sv*a*ng-*ur*	sv*ö*ng	svang-*t*	hungry
l*a*t-*ur*	l*ö*t	lat-*t*	lazy
hamingjus*a*m-*ur*	hamingju-s*ö*m	hamingjusam-*t*	happy
k*a*ld-*ur*	k*ö*ld	kal-*t*	cold

Some irregularities in the declension of adjectives can be explained by assimilation. Assimilation is a process by which a sound changes to become identical with a neighboring sound.

Masculine	Feminine	Neuter	English
dökkhærð-*ur*	dökkhærð	dökkhær*ð*-*t* → dökkhær-*t*	darkhaired
gla*ð*-*ur*	glö*ð*	gla*ð*-*t* → glat-*t*	happy
gó*ð*-*ur*	gó*ð*	go*ð*-*t* → got-*t*	good

In the neuter form of **dökkhærður**, **ð** assimilates with the **t** and disappears because you cannot have the consonant cluster **rðt**. Similarly, the consonant cluster **ðt** becomes **tt** in the neuter forms of the adjectives **glaður** and **góður**.

Note also that in **góður**, the vowel **ó** shifts to a short **o** sound in the neuter form.

Category 2 Adjectives

The second category of adjectives consists of adjectives which have no inflectional ending in masculine but a **t** in neuter. The stem may end either in **r**, **s**, or **ss**:

Category 2 Adjective Endings

Masculine	Feminine	Neuter
–	–	t

There are not many adjectives that follow this pattern, but some of them are very common.

Masculine	Feminine	Neuter	English
stór	stór	stór-*t*	big
skýr	skýr	skýr-*t*	clear
kurteis	kurteis	kurteis-*t*	polite
hress	hress	hress-*t*	healthy, in good spirits

Category 3 Adjectives

Many short, one-syllable adjectives follow this next pattern. Here, we add an **r** in masculine and **tt** in neuter.

Category 3 Adjective Endings

Masculine	Feminine	Neuter
r	–	tt

Masculine	Feminine	Neuter	English
blá-*r*	blá	blá-*tt*	blue
hlý-*r*	hlý	hlý-*tt*	warm
há-*r*	há	há-*tt*	high
ný-*r*	ný	ný-*tt*	new

Category 4 Adjectives

These adjectives have a double **n** in masculine and one **n** in feminine. The first **n** is a part of the stem while the second one is the actual adjective ending. Note also that the **n** in the stem disappears in neuter.

Category 4 Adjective Endings

Masculine	Feminine	Neuter
nn	n	ð

Masculine	Feminine	Neuter	English
feimi*n-n*	feimi*n*	feimi-*ð*	shy
ástfangi*n-n*	ástfangi*n*	ástfangi-*ð*	in love

Category 5 Adjectives

This category is similar to the one above. The first **l** is a part of the stem while the second one is the actual adjective ending. Note that the **l** in the stem disappears in neuter.

Category 5 Adjective Endings

Masculine	Feminine	Neuter
ll	l	ð

Masculine	Feminine	Neuter	English
líti*l-l*	líti*l*	líti-*ð*	little
miki*l-l*	miki*l*	miki-*ð*	great, a lot

Some adjectives ending with **all** in the masculine form go through a vowel shift in feminine because they have an **a** in the stem. Note that the **l** is not deleted in the neuter forms here.

Masculine	Feminine	Neuter	English
gama*l-l*	g*ö*m*ul*	gama*l-t*	old
einsama*l-l*	eins*ö*m*ul*	einsama*l-t*	alone

The prefix ó– in front of adjectives

When the prefix **ó-** is in front of an adjective, the word acquires the opposite meaning. The prefix **ó-** thus functions like the prefixes *un–*, *ill–*, *irr–*, and *dis–* in English:

Positive Adjective		Negative Adjective	
hamingjusamur	happy	óhamingjusamur	unhappy
ábyrgur	responsible	óábyrgur	irresponsible
kurteis	respectful	ókurteis	disrespectful
ánægður	pleased	óánægður	displeased

Countries and adjectives

Most adjectives derived from names of countries fall into Category 1 for adjectives discussed earlier.

Masculine	Feminine	Neuter	English
íslenskur	íslensk	íslenskt	Icelandic
bandarískur	bandarísk	bandarískt	American
danskur	dönsk	danskt	Danish
enskur	ensk	enskt	English
finnskur	finnsk	finnskt	Finnish
franskur	frönsk	franskt	French
færeyskur	færeysk	færeyskt	Faeroese
grænlenskur	grænlensk	grænlenskt	Greenlandic
hollenskur	hollensk	hollenskt	Dutch
kanadískur	kanadísk	kanadískt	Canadian
norskur	norsk	norskt	Norwegian
rússneskur	rússnesk	rússneskt	Russian
sænskur	sænsk	sænskt	Swedish
þýskur	þýsk	þýskt	German

Examples:

Þetta er rússneskur kennari.	This is a Russian teacher.
Þetta er þýsk kona.	This is a German woman.

Note that adjectives referring to countries are spelled with a small letter in Icelandic, not with a capital letter as in English.

Colors

Colors are also adjectives.

Masculine	Feminine	Neuter	English
hvítur	hvít	hvítt	white
svartur	svört	svart	black
rauður	rauð	rautt	red
gulur	gul	gult	yellow
appelsínugulur	appelsínugul	appelsínugult	orange
bleikur	bleik	bleikt	pink
blár	blá	blátt	blue
fjólublár	fjólublá	fjólublátt	purple
grár	grá	grátt	gray
brúnn	brún	brúnt	brown
grænn	græn	grænt	green

Examples:

hvítur hundur	white dog
grátt hár	gray hair

You can also add the prefix **ljós–** *light* or **dökk–** *dark* to the colors:

ljósblá skyrta	light blue blouse
dökkgræn úlpa	dark green winter jacket

The verb combination *að vera búinn að* + infinitive

The verb combination **að vera búinn að** + *infinitive* is used when someone has finished doing something or when something is completed.

Ég er búinn að borða.	I have [already] eaten.

The **búinn** construction has different endings for different genders, in fact the same endings as Category 4 for adjectives, above:

Masculine	Feminine	Neuter
bú*inn*	bú*in*	bú*ið*

Pabbi er bú*inn* að elda pasta.	Dad has cooked pasta.
Stelpan er bú*in* að læra.	The girl has finished studying.

When **búinn** is used without the second verb, it means that the subject of the sentence is over or finished.

Þetta er bú*ið*.	This is over/finished/done.
Maturinn er bú*inn*.	The food is finished.

Æfingar – Exercises

1. Change the gender of the underlined adjective.

a) Ari er <u>íslenskur</u>.   Anna er _____

b) Adam er <u>kanadískur</u>.   Lesley er _____

c) George er _____   Sheila er <u>bandarísk</u>.

d) Timo er _____   Asta er <u>finnsk</u>.
e) Pierre er <u>franskur</u>.   Julie er _____
f) Sven er <u>sænskur</u>.   Inga er _____
g) Helmut er _____   Sabine er <u>þýsk</u>.
h) Jesper er <u>hollenskur</u>.   Julia er _____
i) Hans er <u>austurrískur</u>   Heidi er _____
j) Marek er _____   Janina er <u>pólsk</u>.
k) Alexander er <u>úkraínskur</u>. Natalia er _____

2. **Translate the following sentences.**

This is Erna. She is Icelandic. She was born and raised in Reykjavík.
And this is Ómar. He is an actor. He is not shy. He is always happy.
This is Baldur. He is a historian. He is very shy.

3. **Translate the following phrases. Remember to choose the right gender!**

   a. a yellow glass _____
   b. a brown house _____
   c. black tea _____
   d. green tea _____
   e. a gray television _____
   f. a dark blue book _____

4. **Translate the following sentences using *að vera búinn að*.**

   a. Dad has cooked pasta. (að elda)

   _____

   b. He has finished reading. (að lesa)

   _____

   c. Jeremy has done his homework. (að læra heima)

   _____

   d. Hrafnhildur is done showering. (að fara í sturtu)

   _____

5. Find opposite words.

a.	hlýr	1.	ókurteis
b.	hamingjusamur	2.	kaldur
c.	hvítur	3.	lítill
d.	gamall	4.	óhamingjusamur
e.	kurteis	5.	nýr
f.	stór	6.	leiðinlegur
g.	skemmtilegur	7.	svartur

Lesson 5

Í heimsókn hjá Jeremy

◇◇◇◇◇◇

Visiting Jeremy

Samtal 1: Í heimsókn hjá Jeremy

Hrafnhildur og Gunnar eru í heimsókn hjá Jeremy.

Jeremy:	Velkomin og gangið í bæinn!
Hrafnhildur:	Takk.
Gunnar:	Þakka þér fyrir.
Hrafnhildur:	Svo þú býrð hér.
Jeremy:	Já, hér bý ég.
Hrafnhildur:	Býrðu einn?
Jeremy:	Nei, við erum þrjú sem búum hérna. Ég, Jennifer frá Bretlandi og svo Michelle frá Frakklandi.
Hrafnhildur:	Þetta er stór íbúð.
Jeremy:	Já, við erum með fjögur svefnherbergi, lítið eldhús, stofu og eitt baðherbergi.
Gunnar:	Megum við skoða?
Jeremy:	Já, hérna er eldhúsið. Það er ekki stórt.
Hrafnhildur:	En samt mjög bjart og fallegt.
Jeremy:	Já. Og hér til vinstri er svo stofan.
Gunnar:	Hún er mjög stór og skemmtileg.
Jeremy:	Já, og hér erum við með gamalt sjónvarp.
Hrafnhildur:	Rosalega eruð þið með flott útsýni hérna!
Gunnar:	Já, alveg svakalega!
Jeremy:	Já, við erum mjög heppin með útsýnið.
Jeremy:	Jæja, og hér til hægri er svo svefnherbergið mitt. Þarna er skrifborðið mitt og tölvan mín.
Gunnar:	Og hér er ljósmynd. Hver er þetta?
Jeremy:	Þetta er kærastan mín.
Hrafnhildur:	Nú er það? Hvað heitir hún?
Jeremy:	Hún heitir Erica. Hún ætlar að koma í heimsókn í sumar.

Dialogue 1: Visiting Jeremy

Hrafnhildur and Gunnar are visiting Jeremy.

Jeremy:	Welcome and come on in!
Hrafnhildur:	Thanks.
Gunnar:	Thank you.
Hrafnhildur:	So you live here.
Jeremy:	Yes, I live here.
Hrafnhildur:	Do you live alone?
Jeremy:	No, there are three of us who live here: I, Jennifer from Britain, and Michelle from France.
Hrafnhildur:	This is a big apartment.
Jeremy:	Yes, we have four bedrooms, a small kitchen, a living room, and one bathroom.
Gunnar:	Can we look around?
Jeremy:	Yes, here is the kitchen. It's not very big.
Hrafnhildur:	But still it's very bright and beautiful.
Jeremy:	Yes. And to the left is the living room.
Gunnar:	It's very large and nice.
Jeremy:	Here we have an old TV.
Hrafnhildur:	You guys have a great view here!
Gunnar:	Yes, just fantastic!
Jeremy:	We are very lucky with the view.
Jeremy:	Yes, so here to the right is my bedroom. That's my desk and my computer.
Gunnar:	And here's a photo. Who is that?
Jeremy:	That's my girlfriend.
Hrafnhildur:	Oh yeah? What is her name?
Jeremy:	Her name is Erica. She is planning on coming to visit this summer.

Samtal 2

Jeremy:	Jæja, nú er maturinn tilbúinn. Gjörið þið svo vel og fáið ykkur!
Gunnar:	Kærar þakkir.
Hrafnhildur:	Takk takk!

Þau setjast og fá sér að borða. Jeremy er búinn að elda pasta.

Gunnar:	Mmmmm. Þetta er mjög góður matur.
Hrafnhildur:	Já, Jeremy þú ert sko frábær kokkur!
Jeremy:	Takk. Þetta er nú ekkert merkilegt. Þú veist, bara pasta og smá sósa.
Gunnar:	Jú, þetta er mjög gott. Skál fyrir Jeremy!
Hrafnhildur:	Já, fyrir Jeremy!
Jeremy:	Skál!

Nú eru Gunnar og Hrafnhildur búin að borða.

Jeremy:	Má ekki bjóða ykkur meira?
Hrafnhildur:	Nei takk. Þetta var alveg frábært.
Gunnar:	Já, takk fyrir mig!
Hrafnhildur:	Takk fyrir mig!
Jeremy:	Verði ykkur að góðu.

Dialogue 2

Jeremy: Okay, the food is ready. Help yourselves!

Gunnar: Thanks so much.
Hrafnhildur: Thank you!

They sit and eat. Jeremy has made pasta.

Gunnar: Mmmmm. This is great food.
Hrafnhildur: Yes, Jeremy you are a great cook!
Jeremy: Thank you. This is nothing, though. You know, just some
               pasta and sauce.
Gunnar: It's really good. Cheers for Jeremy!
Hrafnhildur: For Jeremy!
Jeremy: Cheers!

Gunnar and Hrafnhildur have finished eating.

Jeremy: Can I offer you some more?
Hrafnhildur: No, thank you. That was just great.
Gunnar: Yes, thank you so much!
Hrafnhildur: Thank you!
Jeremy: No problem.

Orðaforði – Vocabulary

baðherbergi *n. neu.* bathroom
að borða *v1* to eat
að bjóða *v3* (**ég býð**) to invite
Bretland *n. neu.* Britain
að búa *v5* (**ég bý**) to live
búinn *adj. m.* finished, done
bær *n. m. here:* home
eitt *num. neu.* one
að elda *v1* to cook
ekkert *pron. neu.* nothing
eldhús *n. neu.* kitchen
að fá *v5* (**ég fæ**) to get
fjögur *num. neu.* four
flott *adj. neu.* great
Frakkland *n. neu.* France
gamalt *adj. neu.* old
að ganga *v3* (**ég geng**) to walk
góður *adj. m.* good, tasty
heimsókn *n. f.* visit
heppin *adj. neu. pl.* lucky
hér *adv.* here
hérna *adv.* here
hægri *adj.* right side
íbúð *n. f.* apartment
jú *interj.* yes
jæja *interj.* well! okay!
kokkur *n. m.* cook
kærasta *n. f.* girlfriend
lítið *adj. neu.* small
ljósmynd *n. f.* photography

að mega *v. irr.* may
merkilegt *adj.* remarkable
nú *adv.* now
nú *interj.* oh? or as emphasis *(see examples below)*
pasta *n. neu.* pasta
rosalega *adv.* very, extremely
að setjast *v4 st-form* to sit down
sér *pron. refl.* oneself, themselves
sjónvarp *n. neu.* television
skál *n. f. here:* cheers!
skemmtileg *adj. f.* fun
sko *interj.* (see examples below)
að skoða *v1* to look at, to look around
skrifborð *n. neu.* writing desk
smá *adv.* a bit
sósa *n. f.* sauce
stofa *n. f.* living room
sumar *n. neu.* summer
svakalega *adv.* extremely
svefnherbergi *n. neu.* bedroom
til *prep.* to
tilbúinn *adj. m.* ready
tölva *n. f.* computer
útsýni *n. neu.* view
velkomin *adj. neu. pl.* welcome
vinstri *adj.* left side
þrjú *num. neu.* three
að ætla *v1* to intend

Orðasambönd – Useful expressions

Singular	Plural	Translation
Gakktu í bæinn!	Gangið í bæinn!	Come on in!
Gjörðu svo vel!	Gjörið svo vel!	Help yourself/ go ahead!
Má bjóða þér meira?	Má bjóða ykkur meira?	Would you like some more?

Takk fyrir mig!	Takk fyrir okkur!	Thank you *(for the*
(lit. Thanks for me!)	*(lit. Thanks for us!)*	*dinner)*!
Verði þér að góðu!	Verði ykkur að góðu!	You are welcome!
Skál!	–	Cheers!

The definite article

As you may have noticed, Icelandic has no indefinite article. Icelandic does have a definite article, though, and it is attached to the end of nouns: **gestur** → **gesturinn**, *a guest* → *the guest*. The three grammatical genders each have different articles:

the definite article (the)

Masculine	Feminine	Neuter
(i)nn	(i)n	(i)ð

Nouns ending in a consonant:

Masculine	Feminine	Neuter
maður → maður-*inn*	mynd → mynd-*in*	barn → barn-*ið*
stóll → stóll-*inn*	borg → borg-*in*	blóm → blóm-*ið*
steinn → steinn-*inn*	sól → sól-*in*	borð → borð-*ið*

Nouns ending in a vowel:

Masculine	Feminine	Neuter
lampi → lampi-*nn*	kona → kona-*n*	hjarta → hjarta-*ð*
penni → penni-*nn*	stelpa → stelpa-*n*	súkkulaði → súkkulaði-*ð*

Possessives

The possessives for the first and second person singular are declined according to gender. The rest of the possessives are formed using the genitive form of the personal pronouns (for genitive, see Lesson 14). You do not really need to know which is genitive and which is not, but you should become acquainted with the following pronouns.

SINGULAR Possessive Adjectives

Person	English	Masculine	Feminine	Neuter
1st	my, mine	minn	mín	mitt
2nd	your, yours	þinn	þín	þitt
3rd *m.*	his	hans		
f.	her	hennar		
neu.	its	þess		

Note the different vowels in **m*i*nn** and **m*i*tt** versus **m*í*n** as well as **þ*i*nn** and **þ*i*tt** versus **þ*í*n**!

PLURAL Possessive Adjectives

Person	English	Masculine	Feminine	Neuter
1st	our, ours	okkar		
2nd	your, yours	ykkar		
3rd	their, theirs	þeirra		

Possessives in Icelandic are placed after the nouns they modify, and the nouns themselves are in definite form. This is quite different than English which places possessives before nouns and uses indefinite nouns.

hundurinn *minn*	my dog
tölvan *hans*	his computer
hjartað *þitt*	your heart
barnið *þeirra*	their child

If you want to emphasize the possession, place the possessive before the noun. Note that the Icelandic noun is in indefinite form in this emphasized construction.

Þetta er *mín* bók!   This is *my* book!

Family members and the definite article

Nouns that refer to friends and some members of the family constitute one major exception to the way in which possession is shown. Compare how some family members use the indefinite form while others use the definite:

Indefinite	Definite
mamma mín my mom	**kona*n* mín** my wife
systir mín my sister	**maður*inn* minn** my husband
bróðir minn my brother	**kærast*inn* minn** my boyfriend
pabbi minn my dad	**kærasta*n* mín** my girlfriend
afi minn my grandfather	
amma mín my grandmother	
vinur minn my friend	
vinkona mín my (girl)friend	

Examples:

Amma mín heitir Hrefna.	My grandmother's name is Hrefna.
Kærast*inn* minn heitir Jón.	My boyfriend's name is Jón.

Numbers 1–20

In Lesson 3, you learned about the three different genders of adjectives. The numbers from 1–4 also have different genders.

Numbers 1-4

	Masculine	Feminine	Neuter
1	einn	ein	eitt
2	tveir	tvær	tvö
3	þrír	þrjár	þrjú
4	fjórir	fjórar	fjögur

The following numbers have no gender. Note, however, that in numbers higher than 20 when the last digit is a number from 1 to 4, these numbers will again have gender (see Lesson 10).

Numbers 5-20

5	fimm	13	þrettán
6	sex	14	fjórtán
7	sjö	15	fimmtán
8	átta	16	sextán
9	níu	17	sautján
10	tíu	18	átján
11	ellefu	19	nítján
12	tólf	20	tuttugu

The number *zero* is **núll** in Icelandic and, like numbers higher than four, it does not decline. It is also important to note that it is pronounced with a long *l* sound like **grilla** and not like the *tl*-sound in **sæll** (see the section on pronunciation earlier in this book).

For higher numbers, see Lesson 10.

Choosing the right gender of numbers

Gender of numbers depends on the gender of the objects you are counting. If you are counting *Icelandic money* you use feminine because the Icelandic currency **krónur** *kronas* is a feminine noun (see Lesson 10). If you are counting *dollars* you use masculine because the noun **dollari** *dollar* is a masculine noun. If you are not counting anything specific, you will typically use the masculine form. Note that telephone numbers are masculine and numbers in street addresses are neuter.

Ég bý í Aðalstræti fjögur.   I live at 4 Aðalstræti.
Síminn minn er fimm fimm   My phone number is five five one
einn tveir tveir þrír þrír.   two two three three.

Að ætla að (to intend to) + infinitive

The verb combination **að ætla að** *to intend to* + *infinitive* is used in a way similar to the usage of the verb combination *to be going to* + *infinitive* in English.

Hvað ætlar Hrafnhildur   What is Hrafnhildur going to do?
** að gera?**
Hrafnhildur ætlar að læra.   Hrafnhildur is going to study.

The verb **að ætla** is subject to conjugation while the second verb is always in the infinitive. The verb **ætla** is a regular verb and it conjugates as follows (see **tala** *speak* in Lesson 2):

að ætla (to intend)

Person	Singular			Plural		
1st	ég	ætl-*a*	I intend	við	ætl-*um*	we intend
2nd	þú	ætl-*ar*	you intend	þið	ætl-*ið*	you intend
3rd *m.*	hann		he	þeir		
f.	hún	ætl-*ar*	she intends	þær	ætl-*a*	they intend
neu.	það		it	þau		

Nú, sko, hérna, þú veist, and *jæja*

In the dialogue about visiting Jeremy, there are several words and phrases which are used almost exclusively in spoken language: **nú**, **sko**, **hérna**, **þú veist**, and **jæja**. It is very useful to recognize these words as they play an important role in spoken interaction.

Hérna (here) and *þarna* (there)

These are often used as hesitation markers similar to the way in which English uses *eh* and *uhm*. The last vowel is often prolonged, i.e. **hérnaaa**. Remember this is only in spoken language!

Ég *hérna* hringi á morgun.	I will *eh* call tomorrow.
Þarna, hvað heitirðu?	*Uhm*, what's your name?

Nú

The temporal adverb **nú** *now* has several other nontemporal functions:

1) As an emphatic word when you would use stress in English:

   Hvað er *nú* þetta?   What is THIS?

2) As a discourse marker when someone is telling a long story:

   ... *nú*, svo fór hann   ... well, then he just went home.
   bara heim.

3) As a surprise marker:

   Nú* er það?   Oh really?

Sko

1) When it is used right after the verb, it typically gives emphasis:

   Þú ert *sko* góður kokkur!   You're a good cook *(for sure)*!

2) It can also function like *well* in English:

   Sko*, fyrst fer ég heim.   Well, first I'll go home.

3) It can also function as *y'know* or *you see*:

>**Ég kann ekki íslensku *sko*.**   I don't understand Icelandic,
>   you see.

Þú veist

Þú veist is equivalent to the English *y'know*. The particle is relatively new in Icelandic, and the usage has been increasing in recent years. Sometimes the pronunciation is reduced to **þúst** or even **sst**.

Jæja

The usage of **jæja** is often similar to the usage of *well* in English.

>**Jæja, maturinn er til!**   Well, the food is ready!

Verb-second rule

In Icelandic, the verb is always in *second place* in a sentence. If a sentence begins with something other than a subject, the subject will then follow the verb since the verb must remain in second place.

Subject	Verb	Adverbial	Object	Adverbial
Jeremy	**talar**	**ekki**	**íslensku**	**í dag.**
Jeremy	speaks	not	Icelandic	today.

Adverbial	Verb	Subject	Adverbial	Object
Í dag	**talar**	**Jeremy**	**ekki**	**íslensku.**
Today	speaks	Jeremy	not	Icelandic.

Note that adverbs such as **oft** *often*, **stundum** *sometimes*, and **aldrei** *never* are placed in the same position as **ekki** *not*.

Subject	Verb	Adverbial	Object	Adverbial
Ég	**fer**	**stundum**		**í bíó.**
I	go	sometimes		to the movies.
Ég	**reyki**	**aldrei**	**sígarettur.**	
I	smoke	never	cigarettes.	

Æfingar – Exercises

1. Form the definite.

    a.   Hér er sófi. Er þetta _____ þinn?

    b.   Hér er tölva. Er þetta _____ þín?

    c.   Hér er lykill. Er þetta _____ þinn?

    d.   Hér er íbúð. Er þetta _____ þín?

    e.   Hér er gata. Er þetta _____ þín?

    f.   Hér er eldhús. Er þetta _____ þitt?

    g.   Hér er hundur. Er þetta _____ þinn?

    h.   Hér er rúm. Er þetta _____ þitt?

2. Form the indefinite.

    a.   Þetta er _____ → Þetta er borgin mín.

    b.   Þetta er _____ → Þetta er kisan mín.

    c.   Þetta er _____ → Þetta er húsið mitt.

    d.   Þetta er _____ → Þetta er skyrið mitt.

    e.   Þetta er _____ → Þetta er penninn minn.

3. Write possessive pronouns which correspond to the words in the parentheses.

    a.   Hér er hundurinn _____ (þú)

    b.   Er þetta mamma _____ ? (hún)

    c.   Hér er skólinn _____ (við)

    d.   Þarna er kærastan _____ (ég)

4. Fill in the blanks.

a. Einn plús þrír eru _____ .

b. Tveir plús fimmtán eru _____ .

c. Sjö plús fimm eru _____ .

d. Tólf mínus tveir eru _____ .

e. Sex mínus einn eru _____ .

f. _____ plús einn eru sex.

g. Sjö mínus _____ eru fjórir.

h. Fimm mínus fimm eru _____ .

5. Write down the telephone numbers.

Hvað er síminn hjá þér?
a. Hann er 561 2345

_____

b. Númerið mitt er 431 5675

_____

c. Símanúmerið mitt er 491 4145

_____

6. Spell out the correct numbers in the blanks.

a. Þetta eru _____ krónur. (2)
b. Þetta er _____ króna. (1)
c. Þetta eru _____ dollarar. (3)
d. Þetta eru _____ dollarar. (5)

LESSON 6

Venjulegur dagur

◇◇◇◇◇◇

An ordinary day

Samtal: Venjulegur dagur

Í dag er miðvikudagur. Jeremy er sofandi. Allt í einu hringir síminn og
Jeremy vaknar og kíkir á klukkuna. Klukkan er korter í ellefu. Hann
fer á fætur og svarar í símann.

Jeremy:	Já, halló.
Gunnar:	Góðan daginn. Er Jeremy við?
Jeremy:	Það er hann.
Gunnar:	Blessaður. Varstu sofandi?
Jeremy:	Já, ég var steinsofandi.
Gunnar:	Æi, fyrirgefðu! Klukkan er að verða ellefu. Sefurðu alltaf svona lengi?
Jeremy:	Ekki á hverjum degi. Skólinn byrjar klukkan átta á mánudögum og fimmtudögum. Þá fer ég á fætur klukkan sjö.
Gunnar:	En í dag er miðvikudagur.
Jeremy:	Já einmitt, og á miðvikudögum og föstudögum er enginn skóli. Þá sef ég oft til tíu eða ellefu.
Gunnar:	Hvað gerirðu á miðvikudögum og föstudögum?
Jeremy:	Fyrst fer ég í sturtu og borða morgunmat. Svo læri ég heima. Klukkan tólf borða ég hádegismat. Oftast borða ég heima en stundum fer ég á kaffihús. En þú? Þú ert leikari og vinnur á kvöldin, er það ekki?
Gunnar:	Jú, en ég vinn stundum á kvöldin og stundum á daginn. Við æfum á daginn en svo sýnum við á kvöldin. Á morgun æfum við frá klukkan tíu til hálf tvö, og á föstudaginn sýnum við frá klukkan níu til ellefu. Við ætlum að frumsýna nýtt íslenskt leikrit.
Jeremy:	Er frumsýning á föstudaginn? En spennandi!
Gunnar:	Já, og ég ætla að bjóða þér. Hvað ertu að gera á föstudagskvöldið? Ertu upptekinn?
Jeremy:	Nei, ég er ekki að gera neitt sérstakt á föstudaginn.
Gunnar:	Frábært. Komdu í leikhúsið klukkan korter í átta og ég læt þig fá miða.
Jeremy:	Þakka þér kærlega fyrir. Ég kem!
Gunnar:	Flott, sjáumst á föstudaginn!
Jeremy:	Bless bless!

Dialogue: An ordinary day

Today is Wednesday. Jeremy is asleep. All of a sudden the phone rings and Jeremy wakes up and looks at the clock. It's a quarter to eleven. He gets up and answers the phone.

Jeremy: Yes, hello.

Gunnar: Good day. Is Jeremy there?

Jeremy: This is he.

Gunnar: Hello Jeremy. Were you sleeping?

Jeremy: Yes, I was totally asleep.

Gunnar: Oh, I'm sorry! It's almost eleven o'clock. Do you always sleep in so late?

Jeremy: Not every day. School starts at eight o'clock on Mondays and Thursdays. So I get up then at seven.

Gunnar: And today is Wednesday.

Jeremy: Yes, exactly, and on Wednesdays and Fridays there's no school. I sleep until ten or eleven then.

Gunnar: What do you do on Wednesdays and Fridays?

Jeremy: First I take a shower and eat breakfast. Then I study at home. At twelve I eat lunch. Usually I eat at home, but sometimes I go to a café. What about you? You're an actor so you work in the evenings, isn't that right?

Gunnar: Yes, but I work in the evenings sometimes and sometimes during the day. We rehearse during the day and then have our shows in the evenings. Tomorrow we're going to rehearse from ten until half past one, and on Friday our show is from nine till eleven. We are going to premiere a new Icelandic play.

Jeremy: Is there a premiere on Friday? How exciting!

Gunnar: Yes, and I was planning on inviting you. What are you doing on Friday night? Are you busy?

Jeremy: I am not planning anything specific on Friday.

Gunnar: Great. Come to the playhouse at quarter to eight and I will give you a ticket.

Jeremy: Thank you kindly. I'll be there!

Gunnar: Great! See you on Friday!

Jeremy: Bye bye!

Orðaforði – Vocabulary

alltaf *adv.* always
allt í einu *adv.* suddenly
á hverjum degi *adv.* every day
að bjóða *v5* **(ég býð)** to invite, to offer
að byrja *v1* to start
dagur *n. m.* day
enginn *pron. m.* nobody
einmitt *adv.* exactly
ellefu *num.* eleven
að fara *v4* **(ég fer)** to go
að fara á fætur to get up
að fara í sturtu to take a shower
að frumsýna *v2* to have a premier
frumsýning *n. f.* premier
að fyrirgefa *v3* to forgive
fyrirgefðu *v3 imp.* sorry
fyrst *adv.* first
föstudagskvöld *n. neu.* Friday night
föstudagur *n. m.* Friday
að gera *v2* to do
hádegismatur *n. m.* lunch
heima *adv.* at home
að hringja *v2* to call
kaffihús *n. neu.* café
að kíkja *v2* to have a look
klukka *n. f.* clock
að koma *v3* **(ég kem)** to come
komdu *v3 imp.* come!
korter *n. neu.* quarter

kvöld *n. neu.* evening
að láta *v3* **(ég læt)** to let
leikrit *n. neu.* play
að læra heima to do homework
mánudagur *n. m.* Monday
miði *n. m.* ticket
miðvikudagur *n. m.* Wednesday
á morgun tomorrow
morgunmatur *n. m.* breakfast
neitt *pron. neu.* anything
nýtt *adj. neu.* new
oft *adv.* often
oftast *adv.* usually
sérstakt *adj. neu.* special
sími *n. m.* telephone
sofandi *adj.* sleeping
spennandi *adj.* exciting
steinsofandi *adj.* sleeping very deeply
stundum *adv.* sometimes
sturta *n. f.* shower
sýning *n. f.* show
að sýna *v2* to show
að svara *v1* to answer
upptekinn *adj. m.* busy
að vakna *v1* to wake up
að vera við *v. irr.* to be available
að vinna *v3* to work
þá *adv.* then
að æfa *v2* to practice, to rehearse

Days of the week

Note that the days of the week are not capitalized in Icelandic:

Í dag er	Today is
mánudagur.	Monday.
þriðjudagur.	Tuesday.
miðvikudagur.	Wednesday.
fimmtudagur.	Thursday.
föstudagur.	Friday.
laugardagur.	Saturday.
sunnudagur.	Sunday.

Í dag er þriðjudagur.	Today is Tuesday.
Á morgun er miðvikudagur.	Tomorrow is Wednesday.
Í gær var sunnudagur.	Yesterday was Sunday.

When you want to say that you did something on a particular day, or that you are going to do something on a particular day, you have to use another form of the day *(accusative, definite form)*:

á mánudaginn	on Monday
á þriðjudaginn	on Tuesday
á miðvikudaginn	on Wednesday

Ég ætla í sund á sunnudaginn.	I'm going to the pool on Sunday.
Ég var heima á fimmtudaginn.	I was at home on Thursday.

When you want to say that you do something that recurs the same day every week (as opposed to on a specific day) you use yet another form of the day *(dative, plural)*:

á mánudögum	on Mondays
á þriðjudögum	on Tuesdays
á miðvikudögum	on Wednesdays

Ég vinn á fimmtudögum.	I work Thursdays.
Ég fer í skólann á miðvikudögum.	I go to school on Wednesdays.

Telling time

Icelanders use the twenty-four hour clock when writing schedules or invitations. In conversation, however, people tend to use the twelve-hour clock.

A)   To express full hours:

Note that the noun **klukka** *clock* is feminine, and thus we can also refer to it as **hún** *she*. The number, however, is expressed with a numeral in neuter.

13.00	6.00	12.00
Klukkan er eitt.	**Hún er sex.**	**Klukkan er tólf.**

B) To express half-hours:

12.30	5.30	11.30
Klukkan er hálf eitt.	**Klukkan er hálf sex.**	**Hún er hálf tólf.**

Note that, unlike English, the half-hour is expressed as *before* the hour rather than after the hour, so that 5:30 *five-thirty* is **hálf sex** *half* [before] *six*.

C) To express more precise time—a number of minutes to or past the hour— use **mínútur** (the feminine form for *minutes*) plus **í** *to* or **yfir** *past*:

12.58	19.03
Hún er tvær mínútur í eitt.	**Klukkan er þrjár mínútur yfir sjö.**

3.40	9.10
Klukkan er tuttugu mínútur í fjögur.	**Hún er tíu mínútur yfir níu.**

D) *Quarter to* **korter í** and *quarter past* **korter yfir**:

4.45	14.15	00.15
Klukkan er korter í fimm.	**Klukkan er korter yfir tvö.**	**Hún er korter yfir tólf.**

E) Alternative ways of expressing less than full hours:

1.05
Klukkan er fimm mínútur *gengin* í tvö.
   lit.: The clock has *gone* five minutes towards two.

4.55
Klukkuna *vantar* fimm mínútur í fimm.
   lit.: The clock *lacks* five minutes to five.

Conjugation of verbs in present tense

So far, you have learned the conjugation of four different verbs: **ætla, tala, heita,** and **vera**. **Ætla** and **tala** belong to the first conjugation of verbs *(v1)* while **heita** belongs to the second conjugation *(v2)*. There are three other regular conjugations in present tense and it is now time to look at them. These verbs may prove to be more difficult to learn since they often go through a vowel shift (referred to as the *i-shift*) in the singular. Remember that all verbs have the same endings in the plural.

Category 3 Verbs *(v3)*: *að vinna* (to work)

The third category of verbs conjugates like the verb **að vinna** *to work*. These verbs have no ending in first person singular but add **ur** in second and third person:

Endings for Category 3 Verbs

	Singular Ending	Plural Ending
1ˢᵗ	–	-um
2ⁿᵈ	-ur	-ið
3ʳᵈ	-ur	-a

að vinn-a (to work)

Singular	Plural
ég vinn- I work	**við vinn-*um*** we work
þú vinn-*ur* you work	**þið vinn-*ið*** you work
hann/hún/það vinn-*ur* he/she/it works	**þeir/þær/þau vinn-*a*** they work

að skilj-a (to understand)

Singular	Plural
ég skil I understand	**við skil-j-*um*** we understand
þú skil-*ur* you understand	**þið skil-j-*a*** you understand
hann/hún/það skil-*ur* he/she/it understands	**þeir/þær/þau skil-j-*ið*** they understand

að gang-a (to walk)

Singular	Plural
ég geng- I walk	**við göng-*um*** we walk
þú geng-*ur* you walk	**þið gang-*ið*** you walk
hann/hún/það geng-*ur* he/she/it walks	**þeir/þær/þau gang-*a*** they walk

Note that the *a* sound in **ganga** shifts to an **e** in singular and to an **ö** in first person plural. Vowel shifts will be addressed below.

Category 4 Verbs *(v4)*: *að lesa* (to read)

The fourth category of verbs conjugates like the verb **að lesa** *to read*. The verbs in this category have stems which end in either **s** or **r**. When the stem ends in an **s**, a **t** is added in second person singular, such as in **þú lest** *you read*. When the stem ends in an **r**, on the other hand, an **ð** is added, such as in **þú spyrð** *you ask*.

Endings for Category 4 Verbs

	Singular Ending	Plural Ending
1ˢᵗ	–	-um
2ⁿᵈ	-ð/t	-ið
3ʳᵈ	–	-a

að les-a (to read)

Singular	Plural
ég les- I read	við les-*um* we read
þú les-*t* you read	þið les-*ið* you read
hann/hún/það les he/she/it reads	þeir/þær/þau les-*a* they read

að spyrj-a (to ask)

Singular	Plural
ég spyr- I ask	við spyr-j-*um* we ask
þú spyr-*ð* you ask	þið spyr-j-*ið* you ask
hann/hún/það spyr he/she/it asks	þeir/þær/þau spyr-j-*a* they ask

að far-a (to go)

Singular	Plural
ég fer- I go	við för-*um* we go
þú fer-*ð* you go	þið far-*ið* you go
hann/hún/það fer he/she/it goes	þeir/þær/þau far-*a* they go

Only a few verbs follow this pattern. Some of these verbs, however, are very frequent, such as the verbs in the charts above. It is very useful to memorize these verbs, especially the verb **að fara**!

Note that due to vowel shifts, the **a** in **fara** shifts to an **e** in singular and to an **ö** in first person plural (see discussion below).

Category 5 Verbs *(v5)*: *að búa* (to live)

The fifth category of verbs conjugates like the verb **að búa** *to live*. The stem of these verbs ends with a vowel (or a **j**). Note that some of these verbs do not have a final **a** in the infinitive, such as **að þvo** *to wash* and **að fá** *to get*.

Endings for Category 5 Verbs

	Singular Ending	Plural Ending
1st	–	**-um**
2nd	**-rð**	**-ið**
3rd	**-r**	**-a**

að þvo (to wash)

Singular	Plural
ég þvæ- I wash	**við þvo-*um*** we wash
þú þvæ-*rð* you wash	**þið þvo-*ið*** you wash
hann/hún/það þvæ-*r* he/she/it washes	**þeir/þær/þau þvo** they wash

að fá (to get)

Singular	Plural
ég fæ- I get	**við fá-*um*** we get
þú fæ-*rð* you get	**þið fá-*ið*** you get
hann/hún/það fæ-*r* he/she/it gets	**þeir/þær/þau fá** they get

að bú-a (to live)

Singular	Plural
ég bý- I live	**við bú-*um*** we live
þú bý-*rð* you live	**þið bú-*ið*** you live
hann/hún/það bý-*r* he/she/it lives	**þeir/þær/þau bú-*a*** they live

Note the vowel shifts (see discussion below).

An overview of verb conjugation in the present tense

You have now seen all the regular verb categories in present tense, and it is time to compare them all in one chart:

Person		1. að tala (to talk)	2. að heita (to be called)	3. að vinna (to work)	4. að fara (to go)	5. að búa (to live)
1ˢᵗ	ég I	a	i	–	–	–
2ⁿᵈ	þú you	ar	ir	ur	ð/t	rð
3ʳᵈ	hann/hún/það he/she/it	ar	ir	ur	–	r
1ˢᵗ	við we	um				
2ⁿᵈ	þið you *pl.*	ið				
3ʳᵈ	þeir/þær/þau they *m./f./neu.*	a				

As the table illustrates, the verbs follow the same pattern in the plural. It is only the singular that you may have some difficulties memorizing in the beginning. It is also useful to remember that most verbs in Icelandic follow the first three patterns. The latter two, however, include some very common verbs. In the glossary, verbs are referred to by numbers: *v1* means that the verb conjugates like the verb **tala**, *v2* means that it conjugates like the verb **heita**, etc. By knowing what pattern the verb follows, you should be able to conjugate the verb yourself.

Some additional rules for verb conjugation

1. U-shift

When there is an **a** in the stem of the infinitive, such as in **tala** *speak*, the *a* sound shifts to **ö** in first person plural **við tölum** *we talk*. The **u** in the inflectional ending -**um** colors the *a* sound in the verb stem.

2. I-shift

In Categories 3 to 5, there is often a vowel shift in the singular. Due to historical reasons, this shift is called the *i*-shift, even though the letter **i** is not necessarily involved. Note that the *i*-shift does not occur in the plural. In the plural, the vowel is the same as in the infinitive (see the conjugation of **fara** and **búa** in the charts above).

These shifts have a certain pattern, which is listed below:

Sound in infinitive	Changes to	Example	English
a	e	að fara → ég fer	to go
ö	e	að stökkva → ég stekk	to jump
o	e	að sofa → ég sef	to sleep
o	æ	að þvo → ég þvæ	to wash
ó	æ	að róa → ég ræ	to row
á	æ	að fá → ég fæ	to get
ú	ý	að búa → ég bý	to live
jú	ý	að fljúga → ég flýg	to fly
jó	ý	að bjóða → ég být	to invite
au	ey	að hlaupa → ég hleyp	to run
já	é	að sjá → ég sé	to see

The conjugation of the first person singular will be given in the vocabulary list when a verb is subject to the *i*-shift:

að búa *v5* (ég bý)	to live
að taka *v3* (ég tek)	to take

Note that sometimes the same verb can be subject to both the *u*-shift and the *i*-shift, e.g. **að fara** in the table above.

3. *J* in infinitive disappears in singular

If there is a **j** in the final syllable of the infinitive, such as in **að skilja** *to understand*, the **j** disappears in singular but in plural it appears again. Note, however, that when the stem of the verb ends in a **g** or **k** (as in **að segja**), there is no **j** in second person plural (**þið segið**).

Person		að skilja to understand	að segja to say, to tell	að reykja to smoke
1st	ég I	skil	seg-*i*	reyk-*i*
2nd	þú you	skil-*ur*	seg-*ir*	reyk-*ir*
3rd	hann/hún/það he/she/it	skil-*ur*	seg-*ir*	reyk-*ir*

1ˢᵗ *pl.*	við we	skil-j-*um*	seg-j-*um*	reyk-j-*um*
2ⁿᵈ *pl.*	þið you	skil-j-*ið*	seg-*ið*	reyk-*ið*
3ʳᵈ *pl.*	þeir/þær/þau they *m./f./neu.*	skil-j-*a*	seg-j-*a*	reyk-j-*a*

Expressing the future

In Icelandic, the future tense is usually expressed with normal present-tense verbs.

Ég tala við þig í kvöld.   I will talk with you tonight.
Ég fer á morgun.   I will go tomorrow.

Æfingar – Exercises

1. **Fill in the blanks.**

borða *v1*
a. Hrafnhildur _____ morgunmat klukkan sjö.
b. Við _____ morgunmat klukkan átta.
c. Hrafnhildur og Gunnar _____ skyr.

læra *v2*
d. Ég _____ íslensku.
e. Hún _____ alltaf frá tvö til þrjú.
f. Hrafnhildur og Gunnar _____ ensku.
g. Hvað ert þú að _____?

vinna *v3*
h. Ég _____ frá átta til fimm.
i. Hún _____ frá sjö til fjögur.
j. Hrafnhildur og Gunnar _____ í dag.

fara *v4*

k. Þú _____ heim í dag.

l. Við _____ í bíó klukkan níu.

m. Ég _____ í sturtu.

n. Þið _____ í vinnuna klukkan hálf átta.

búa *v5*

o. Hrafnhildur og Gunnar _____ á Íslandi.

p. Ég _____ í Reykjavík.

q. Þið _____ í Bandaríkjunum.

skilja (remember the j-rule!) *v3*

r. Mamma _____ mig ekki!

s. Við _____ íslensku.

t. Hver _____ ensku hér?

u. Anna og Gunni _____ frönsku.

v. Þú _____ mig ekki.

w. Hafliði _____ ensku.

x. Ég _____ íslensku og dönsku.

y. Ferðamaðurinn _____ ekki íslensku.

z. Íslendingar _____ oft ensku.

2. **Look at the time and answer the questions.**

a. Hvað er klukkan?   15.00

   _____

b. Fyrirgefðu, gætirðu sagt mér hvað klukkan er?   12.30

   _____

c. Fyrirgefðu, hvað er klukkan?   7.45

   _____

d. Hvað er klukkan núna?   11.15

   _____

e. Hvað er klukkan?   2.57

   _____

3. Fill in the names of the days in the right form.

a. Í dag er _____ (Tuesday).

b. Ég fer í skólann á _____ og _____
_____ (Mondays, Fridays).

c. Hann ætlar í bíó á _____ (Sunday).

d. Gunnar fer í heimsókn til Jeremys á _____
(Saturday).

e. Hrafnhildur eldar mat á _____ og
_____ (Tuesdays, Thursdays).

f. Á morgun er _____ (Wednesday).

g. Hvar verður þú á _____ (Tuesday)?

4. Translate the following sentences (spell out the times).

a. Where is Gunnar? He is at home.

_____

b. I go home at 5:30.

_____

c. Mom is not at home on Saturdays.

_____

d. I sleep until 11:00 on Sundays.

_____

e. I'm going out at 9:30.

_____

f. We are going to the theater on Wednesday night.

_____

LESSON 7

Ferðamenn í Reykjavík

◇◇◇◇◇

Tourists in Reykjavik

Samtal: Ferðamenn í Reykjavík

Jeremy:	Foreldrar mínir eru að koma í heimsókn í næstu viku. Hvert á ég að fara með þau?
Hrafnhildur:	Bíddu nú við. Það eru mörg áhugaverð söfn í Reykjavík, til dæmis Þjóðminjasafnið og Listasafn Íslands.
Jeremy:	Góð hugmynd! Veistu hvað kostar inn?
Hrafnhildur:	Nei, ég veit það bara ekki. Ekki svo mikið held ég.
Hrafnhildur:	Og þú mátt ekki gleyma að fara í Þjóðmenningarhúsið. Þar er hægt að kíkja á handritin.
Jeremy:	Er hægt að skoða þau?
Hrafnhildur:	Já, auðvitað! Og svo er náttúrulega hægt að fara á hestbak.
Jeremy:	Hestbak? Mamma og pabbi eru of hrædd til að fara á hestbak.
Hrafnhildur:	Nei nei, íslenskir hestar eru mjög litlir.
Jeremy:	Eru íslenskir hestar minni en amerískir hestar?
Hrafnhildur:	Já, þeir eru miklu minni.
Jeremy:	Ég verð að athuga það.
Hrafnhildur:	Já, mjög margir ferðamenn fara á hestbak. Svo fara líka margir í hvalaskoðun.
Jeremy:	Það er spennandi! Hvað kostar í hvalaskoðun?
Hrafnhildur:	Ég hef ekki hugmynd!
Jeremy:	Eru ferðir alla daga?
Hrafnhildur:	Já, það eru ferðir tvisvar eða þrisvar á dag. Það er ferð klukkan hálf tíu og svo aftur klukkan eitt. Stundum er líka ferð klukkan korter í fimm.
Jeremy:	En ef mamma og pabbi vilja fara í búðir? Hvert á ég að fara með þau?
Hrafnhildur:	Það er skemmtilegast að vera í miðbænum. Það eru mjög margar búðir á Laugaveginum, til dæmis fatabúðir, bókabúðir og minjagripabúðir.
Jeremy:	Hvað eru eiginlega margir íbúar í Reykjavík?
Hrafnhildur:	Um það bil hundrað þúsund.

Dialogue: Tourists in Reykjavik

Jeremy:	My parents are coming to visit next week. Where should I go with them?
Hrafnhildur:	Let's see. There are a lot of interesting museums in Reykjavik, for example the National Museum or The National Art Gallery.
Jeremy:	Good idea! Do you know how much it costs to go?
Hrafnhildur:	No, I don't know. Not so much, I think.
Hrafnhildur:	And you cannot forget to go to the Culture House. You can see the saga manuscripts there.
Jeremy:	Is it possible to look at those?
Hrafnhildur:	Yes, of course! And also you can go horseback riding.
Jeremy:	Horseback riding? My mom and dad are afraid of going horseback riding.
Hrafnhildur:	No, no, Icelandic horses are very small.
Jeremy:	Are Icelandic horses smaller than American horses?
Hrafnhildur:	Yes, a lot smaller.
Jeremy:	I have to look into that.
Hrafnhildur:	A lot of travelers try horseback riding. And a lot of people also go whale watching.
Jeremy:	That's exciting! How much is it to go whale watching?
Hrafnhildur:	I have no idea!
Jeremy:	Are there tours everyday?
Hrafnhildur:	Yes, the tours leave twice or three times a day. There's a tour at nine-thirty and again one at one. Sometimes there's also a tour at four-forty-five.
Jeremy:	And if my parents want to go shopping? Where should I go with them?
Hrafnhildur:	It's best downtown. There are a lot of shops on Laugavegur: clothing stores, book stores, and souvenir shops for example.
Jeremy:	How many people live in Reykjavik actually?
Hrafnhildur:	Approximately a hundred thousand.

Jeremy:	Bara hundrað þúsund?
Hrafnhildur:	Já, en ef maður telur allt höfuðborgarsvæðið með þá eru þeir um hundrað og níutíu þúsund.
Jeremy:	Vá, Reykjavík er ekki stór borg!
Hrafnhildur:	Nei, það er satt. Hún er frekar lítil. En hér er samt nóg um að vera!

Jeremy:	Only a hundred thousand?
Hrafnhildur:	Yes, but if you count the area surrounding the city there are about a hundred and ninety thousand.
Jeremy:	Wow, Reykjavik is not a very big city!
Hrafnhildur:	No, that's true. It's rather small. But there's enough going on!

Orðaforði – Vocabulary

að athuga *v1* to check, look into
aftur *adv.* again
auðvitað *adv.* of course
áhugaverð *adj. neu. pl.* interesting
bíddu nú við *v. imp.* wait a moment
bókabúð *n. f.* book store
búð *n. f.* store
eiginlega *adv.* actually
fatabúð *n. f.* clothing store
ferð *n. f.* trip
ferðamaður *n. m.* tourist
foreldrar *n. m. pl.* parents
frekar *adv.* rather
að gleyma *v2* to forget
góð *adj. f.* good
að halda *v3* **(ég held)** to think
handrit *n. neu* manuscripts *(of the Sagas)*
hestbak *n. neu.* horseback
að fara á hestbak to go horseback riding
hestur *n. m.* horse
hrædd *adj. neu. pl.* scared
hugmynd *n. f.* idea
hvalaskoðun *n. f.* whale watching
höfuðborgarsvæðið *n. neu.* Reykjavik and the surrounding area
að kosta *v1* to cost
íbúi *n. m.* inhabitant
inn *adv.* in

maður *n. m.* man, one *(impersonal)*
mamma *n. f.* mom
með *prep.* with
miðbær *n. m.* downtown
mikið *adv.* much
miklu *adv.* much *(used in comparative)*
minjagripabúð *n. f.* souvenir shop
minni *adj.* smaller
mínir *pron. m. pl.* my
náttúrulega *adv.* naturally, of course
nóg *adv.* enough
næsta *adj. f.* next
of *adv. adj.* too
pabbi *n. m.* dad
safn *n. neu.* museum
samt *adv.* still
satt *adj. neu.* true
skemmtilegast *adj. neu.* most fun
söfn *n. neu. pl., see* **safn**
að skoða *v1* to look at
að telja *v3* **(ég tel)** to count
tvisvar *adv.* twice
vá *interj.* wow
að vera hægt to be possible
að vita *v4* **(ég veit)** to know
Þjóðminjasafnið *n. neu.* The National Museum
Þjóðmenningarhúsið *n. neu.* The Culture House
þrisvar *adv.* three times

Orðasambönd – Useful expressions

Viltu koma …
  á safn?
  á kaffihús?
  á pöbb?
  í leikhús?
  í bíó?
  í gönguferð?

Do you want to go …
  to a museum?
  to a café?
  to a bar?
  to the theater?
  to the movies?
  for a walk?

Já, endilega!	Yes, certainly!
Já, það er góð hugmynd!	Yes, that's a good idea!
Ég veit það ekki.	I don't know.
Nei, ég held ekki.	No, I don't think so.
Því miður þá kemst ég ekki.	Unfortunately, I can't.

Weak and strong nouns

Nouns can be either weak or strong. Weak or strong are just designations and have nothing to do with the relative strength or meaning of nouns.

Weak nouns end in **i** in masculine and **a** in feminine and neuter:

Weak Masculine:
pabb-*i* dad   **frænd-*i*** uncle   **kennar-*i*** teacher

Weak Feminine:
mamm-*a* mom   **kis-*a*** kitty   **tölv-*a*** computer

Weak Neuter:
hjart-*a* heart   **eyr-*a*** ear

Strong nouns end in a consonant in masculine and feminine. In neuter, strong nouns end in a consonant or a vowel other than **a**:

Strong Masculine:
hund-*ur* dog   **stein-*n*** stone
stól-*l* chair   **skó-*r*** shoe

Strong Feminine:
borg city   **bók** book

Neuter:
blóm flower   **hlé** pause
barn child   **te** tea
tré tree

Plural of nouns

In order to be able to add the plural ending, you first have to know how to find the stem of a noun. The following chart shows a few nouns and how to find their stems:

	Masculine	Feminine	Neuter
Ending in a consonant	disk-ur → disk stól-l → stól stein-n → stein bæ-r → bæ	sveit → sveit borg → borg	barn → barn blóm → blóm
Ending in a vowel	pabb-i → pabb lamp-i → lamp	task-a → task tölv-a → tölv	aug-a → aug hjart-a → hjart

To form the plural, you add an ending to the stem. The following table shows the most common plural endings for each gender.

	Masculine	Feminine	Neuter
Strong nouns	ar or ir	ir	–
Weak nouns	ar	ur	u

Plural of masculine nouns

Most masculine nouns form the plural by adding the ending **ar** to the stem. This is true for weak as well as strong nouns.

Singular	Plural
disk-*ur* CD, plate	disk-*ar* CDs, plates
penn-*i* pen	penn-*ar* pens

However, some strong masculine nouns add **ir** instead of **ar**. There is no obvious rule to distinguish between nouns that add **ar** and those which add **ir**. Thus, you sometimes have to look the word up in the vocabulary list to find the plural.

Singular	Plural
gest-*ur* guest	gest-*ir* guests
vin-*ur* friend	vin-*ir* friends

When there is an **ö** in the stem of the noun, and the plural ending is **ir**, the plural has a vowel shift in the stem:

Singular	Plural
fjörð-ur fjord	**firð-ir** fjords
kött-ur cat	**kett-ir** cats

Plural of feminine nouns

Strong feminine nouns, i.e. nouns ending in consonants, typically form the plural by adding **ir** to the stem:

Singular	Plural
borg city	**borg-*ir*** cities
búð shop	**búð-*ir*** shops

When there is an **ö** in the stem of a singular feminine noun, the noun will go through a vowel shift in the plural:

Singular	Plural
gjöf gift	**gjaf-*ir*** gifts
sögn verb	**sagn-ir** verbs
töf delay	**taf-ir** delays

Nouns ending in **a** form the plural by adding **ur** to the stem:

Singular	Plural
klukk-*a* clock	**klukk-*ur*** clocks
kon-*a* woman	**kon-*ur*** women

When there is an **a** in the stem of a singular feminine noun, the noun will go through a vowel shift in the plural:

Singular	Plural
task-*a* bag	**tösk-*ur*** bags
kann-*a* mug	**könn-*ur*** mugs

Plural of neuter nouns

Neuter nouns ending in a consonant do not have any ending in the plural. Thus, you will have to let the context tell you whether the singular or plural form is being used:

Singular	Plural
blóm flower	**blóm** flowers
hús house	**hús** houses

The same applies for neuter nouns that end with a vowel other than **a**. The plural and singular forms are the same. Remember that the vowel here is a part of the stem:

Singular	Plural
veski wallet	**veski** wallets
bindi tie	**bindi** ties
tré tree	**tré** trees

When there is an **a** in the stem of a singular neuter noun, the noun will go through a vowel shift in the plural. This is known as the **u**-shift even though there is no **u** added to the noun:

Singular	Plural
barn child	**börn** children
land country	**lönd** countries

Neuter nouns ending in an **a** form the plural by adding **u** to the stem:

Singular	Plural
eyr-*a* ear	**eyr-***u* ears
lung-*a* lung	**lung-***u* lungs

They can also have a vowel shift when the stem vowel of the singular form is an **a**:

Singular	Plural
hjart-*a* heart	**hjört-***u* hearts

Nouns with no plural

Some nouns occur only in singular, for example the neuter noun **fólk** *people* and many uncountable nouns such as **mjólk** *milk*, **kaffi** *coffee*, and **matur** *food*.

Common irregular plural forms

Note that the endings listed above are only some of the most common plural endings and there are some endings not mentioned here which you will eventually come across. As an example, you may have noticed the plural of the feminine noun **æfing** *exercise* is **æfingar**. The plural ending for feminine nouns ending with **ing** is **ar**.

Furthermore, some of the oldest and most frequently occurring words in Icelandic have irregular plurals:

Irregular Masculine Plural Nouns

maður man	→	**menn** men
sonur son	→	**synir** sons
bróðir brother	→	**bræður** brothers
skór shoe	→	**skór** shoes

Irregular Feminine Plural Nouns

bók book	→	**bækur** books
dóttir daughter	→	**dætur** daughters
systir sister	→	**systur** sisters

Most irregularities can be explained by historical reasons and phonological rules.

How many ... are there here?

The pronoun **margir** *many* changes depending upon the gender of the noun which it modifies:

marg/ir *many*

	Masculine	Feminine	Neuter
Singular	marg-*ur*	m*ö*rg	marg-*t*
Plural	marg-*ir*	marg-*ar*	m*ö*rg

Examples:

margir menn	many men
margar konur	many women
mörg börn	many children

You can use the singular forms of **margir** in some circumstances. For now, we will show only one:

margt fólk	many people *(neu., sing.)*

Use the following to ask *how many?*:

Masculine:

Hvað eru margir hér?	How many people are there here?
Hvað eru margir bílar hér?	How many cars are there here?

Feminine:

Hvað eru margar konur hér?	How many women are there here?

Neuter:

Hvað eru mörg börn hér?	How many children are there here?

Note that the syntax for this phrasing is different than in English. In Icelandic, remember that the verb always has to be in second place. Note also that Icelandic uses **hvað** *what* to ask *how many*. You say literally *what many*. Also note that when the noun is absent such as in the example '**Hvað eru margir hér?**' the default interpretation is 'How many *people* are there here?'

Adjectives ending in *–andi*

Some adjectives are formed from verbs and have the ending **andi**. They do not decline in gender.

að lifa	to live	→	**lifandi tónlist**	live music
að sofa	to sleep	→	**sofandi maður**	sleeping man

Æfingar – Exercises

1. **Find the plural form for the following nouns:**

   a. pabbi   _____
   b. taska   _____
   c. tölva   _____
   d. borð   _____
   e. hnífur   _____
   f. kort   _____
   g. lag   _____
   h. söngvari   _____
   i. bíll   _____
   j. Kanadamaður   _____
   k. köttur   _____

2. **Find the singular form for the following nouns:**

   a. glös   _____
   b. pennar   _____
   c. börn   _____
   d. kennarar   _____
   e. kisur   _____
   f. lönd   _____
   g. peningar   _____
   h. krónur   _____
   i. dollarar   _____

3. **Fill in the blanks with _margir, margar, mörg_:**

   a. Hvað eru _____ söfn í Reykjavík?
   b. Hvað eru _____ konur í Reykjavík?
   c. Hvað eru _____ íbúar í Reykjavík?
   d. Hvað eru _____ Íslendingar hér?

4. Translate:

a.   How many houses are there here?

_____

b.   How many children are there here?

_____

c.   How many horses are there here?

_____

d.   How many people are there here?

_____

Lesson 8

Á leið í útilegu

◇◇◇◇◇

Going camping

Samtal 1: Á leið í útilegu

Í dag er föstudagur og Hrafnhildur og Gunnar eru að fara í útilegu.
Þau ætla að keyra um Suðurland og tjalda í Skaftafelli um helgina. Nú
eru þau að pakka.

Gunnar:	Jæja, eigum við ekki að fara að drífa okkur? Erum við ekki með allt?
Hrafnhildur:	Bíddu aðeins, við skulum skoða þetta.
Hrafnhildur:	Hér eru tveir svefnpokar, tveir bakpokar og tvær dýnur. Gunnar, það vantar tjaldið!
Gunnar:	Nú, er það? Ég er búinn að setja það í bílinn.
Hrafnhildur:	Nei, tjaldið er ekki hér.
Gunnar:	Jæja, ég skal fara og ná í það.

Gunnar fer og nær í tjaldið.

Hrafnhildur:	Hvað ætlum við að borða í kvöld? Það er ekki hægt að kaupa mat í Skaftafelli. Við verðum að taka nesti.
Gunnar:	Ég er búinn að útbúa nesti. Hér eru átta samlokur, harðfiskur, þrjú græn epli, þrjár appelsínur, tveir súpupakkar, fjórar túnfisksdósir, pínu pasta og tvær rauðvínsflöskur.
Hrafnhildur:	Frábært!
Gunnar:	Svo eru hér tveir rauðir diskar, tvær rauðar skálar og tvö rauð glös.
Hrafnhildur:	Flott. Og svo eru hér tveir gafflar, tveir hnífar og tvær skeiðar.

Dialogue 1: Going camping

Today is Friday and Hrafnhildur and Gunnar are going camping. They are going to drive along the south coast and put up a tent in Skaftafell. Now they are packing.

Gunnar:	Well, shouldn't we get going? Do we have everything?

Hrafnhildur:	Just a moment, let's check it out.
Hrafnhildur:	Here are two sleeping bags, two backpacks and two mattresses. Gunni, there is no tent!
Gunnar:	Oh, really? I put it in the car.
Hrafnhildur:	No, the tent is not here.
Gunnar:	Oh well, I will go and get it.

Gunnar goes and gets the tent.

Hrafnhildur:	What are we going to eat tonight? We can't buy food in Skaftafell. We have to bring food.
Gunnar:	I have prepared some food. Here we have eight sandwiches, dried fish, three green apples, three oranges, two instant soups, four tins of tuna, a bit of pasta and two bottles of red wine.
Hrafnhildur:	Great!
Gunnar:	And then we have two red plates, two red bowls, and two red glasses.
Hrafnhildur:	Good. And here we have two forks, two knives and two spoons.

Samtal 2

Gunnar og Hrafnhildur keyra í Skaftafell. Klukkan er orðin
átta þegar þau koma á tjaldstæðið. Þau fara strax að tjalda og bera
dótið inn í tjaldið. Þegar þau eru búin að því setjast þau
inn í tjald.

Hrafnhildur:	Gunnar, ég er ofboðslega svöng. Hvar eru samlokurnar?
Gunnar:	Samlokurnar eru þarna og eplin og appelsínurnar líka.
Hrafnhildur:	Vilt þú ekki fá þér eitthvað að borða?
Gunnar:	Nei takk, ég er ekkert svangur. En mér er mjög kalt. Hvar eru vettlingarnir mínir og sokkarnir?
Hrafnhildur:	Hér eru rauðir vettlingar. Eru þetta vettlingarnir þínir?
Gunnar:	Já, þetta eru vettlingarnir mínir.
Hrafnhildur:	En sokkarnir þínir eru ekki hér. Þetta er mínir.

Nú er klukkan orðin tólf á miðnætti. Gunnar og Hrafnhildur eru orðin
mjög þreytt og þau ætla að fara að sofa.

Gunnar:	Hrafnhildur, hvar eru tannburstarnir?
Hrafnhildur:	Æi, Gunnar, þeir eru heima. Förum bara að sofa. Góða nótt, elskan.
Gunnar:	Góða nótt, ástin mín.

Dialogue 2

Gunnar and Hrafnhildur drive to Skaftafell. It is eight o'clock when they come to the camping site. They immediately start putting up the tent and carrying stuff into the tent. When they are done they sit down in the tent.

Hrafnhildur:	Gunnar, I am terribly hungry. Where are the sandwiches?
Gunnar:	The sandwiches are there and the apples and the oranges too.
Hrafnhildur:	Don't you want to grab something to eat?
Gunnar:	No thanks, I'm not hungry. But I'm very cold. Where are my mittens and my socks?
Hrafnhildur:	Here are red mittens. Are these your mittens?
Gunnar:	Yes, these are my mittens.
Hrafnhildur:	But your socks are not here. These are mine.

Now the time is twelve midnight. Gunnar and Hrafnhildur are very tired and are going to go to sleep.

Gunnar:	Hrafnhildur, where are the toothbrushes?
Hrafnhildur:	Oh, Gunnar, they are at home. Let's just go to sleep. Good night, darling.
Gunnar:	Good night, my love.

Orðaforði – Vocabulary

aðeins *adv.* a bit
appelsína *n. f.* orange
ást *n. f.* love
bakpoki *n. m.* backpack
bíll *n. m.* car
að drífa okkur to hurry up
dýna *n. f.* mattress
að eiga *v. irr.* to be supposed to
elska *n. f.* darling
epli *n. neu.* apple
gaffall *n. m.* fork
glas *n. neu.* glass
glös *n. neu. pl., see* **glas**
harðfiskur *n. m.* hardfish/dried fish
   (Icelandic specialty)
að keyra *v2* to drive
miðnætti *n. neu.* midnight
að ná *v5* **(ég næ)** to get, fetch
nesti *n. neu.* bagged lunch, provisions
ofboðslega *adv.* terribly
okkur *pron. dat. pl.* we *(us)*
að pakka *v1* to pack
rauð *adj. neu. pl.* red
rauðir *adj. m. pl.* red

rauðvínsflaska *n. f.* bottle of red wine
samloka *n. f.* sandwich
að setja *v3* to put
skál *n. f.* bowl
skeið *n. f.* spoon
að skoða *v1* to look at, to check
skulu *v. irr.* shall
sokkur *n. m.* socks
Suðurland *n. neu.* the south part of
   Iceland
súpupakki *n. m.* instant soup
svefnpoki *n. m.* sleeping bag
tannbursti *n. m.* toothbrush
að tjalda *v1* to camp
tjald *n. neu.* tent
tjaldstæði *n. neu.* camping site
túnfisksdós *n. f.* can of tuna
um helgina during the weekend
útbúa *v5* to prepare
útilega *n. f.* camping trip
að vanta *v1* to lack, to need
að vera hægt to be possible
að vera með to have (to own)
vettlingur *n. m.* mitten

Orðasambönd – Useful expressions

Directions:

norður	north
suður	south
austur	east
vestur	west

Ég er að fara norður.	I'm going north.
Ég ætla vestur.	I'm going west.
Ég ætla suður á morgun.	I'm going south tomorrow *(this usually implies to Reykjavik).*

The directions are used to refer to different parts of Iceland:

Suðurland	the southern part of Iceland
Norðurland	the northern part of Iceland
Austurland	the eastern part of Iceland
Austfirðir	the east fjords
Vesturland	the western part of Iceland
Vestfirðir	the west fjords
hálendið	the highland, middle part of Iceland

Við ætlum að keyra um hálendið.	We are going to drive on the highland.
Ég bý á Austurlandi.	I live in eastern Iceland.
Ég bý á Vestfjörðum.	I live in the west fjords.

Note that these parts of the country are capitalized, except for **hálendið** which is a definite form.

Vowel deletion in plural nouns

In strong nouns that end with a vowel followed by **ll** or **nn** in singular, the last vowel may be deleted in the plural. Take for instance the word **gaffall** *fork*. It is a masculine noun and, like other masculine nouns which end in **double l**, you have to drop the second **l** to isolate the stem. The stem is thus **gaffal**. When you then add the masculine plural ending to the stem **ar**, the unstressed **a** disappears: **gaff/*a*/lar → gafflar**.

Singular		Plural
lykill key	→	**lyklar** keys
trefill scarf	→	**treflar** scarves
gaffall fork	→	**gafflar** forks
jökull glacier	→	**jöklar** glaciers

This rule applies to a few strong nouns ending with **ill**, **all**, **ull**, **inn**, **ann**, and **unn**.

Plural with the definite article

Changing a singular noun to plural does not only affect the noun itself, it also affects the definite article. The following chart shows the singular and plural of the definite article:

Singular & Plural of the Definite Article

	Masculine	Feminine	Neuter
Singular	(i)nn	(i)n	(i)ð
Plural	nir	nar	(i)n

Examples:

Singular		Plural
hund-ur-*inn* the dog	→	**hund-ar-*nir*** the dogs
skól-i-*nn* the school	→	**skól-ar-*nir*** the schools
búð-*in* the store	→	**búð-ir-*nar*** the stores
stúlk-a-*n* the girl	→	**stúlk-ur-*nar*** the girls
blóm-*ið* the flower	→	**blóm-*in*** the flowers
eyr-a-*ð* the ear	→	**eyr-u-*n*** the ears

The plural definite for the word **maður** *man* is irregular. To say *the men*, the form in Icelandic is **menn-*irnir***. The declension of the noun **maður** is given in the grammar summary at the back of the book.

Plural possessives

The plural of possessives **minn** *my* and **þinn** *your* follows a pattern which is similar to the plural of the definite article.

minn (my) and þinn (your)

	Masculine	Feminine	Neuter
Singular	minn/þinn	mín/þín	mitt/þitt
Plural	mín-*ir*/þín-*ir*	mín-*ar*/þín-*ar*	mín/þín

Examples:

Singular		Plural
skól-i-*nn* minn my school	→	skól-ar-*nir* mín-*ir* my schools
hund-ur-*inn* þinn your dog	→	hund-ar-*nir* þín-*ir* your dogs
klukk-a-*n* mín my clock	→	klukk-ur-*nar* mín-*ar* my clocks
borg-*in* þín your city	→	borg-ir-*nar* þín-*ar* your cities
blóm-*ið* þitt your flower	→	blóm-*in* þín your flowers

Remember that possessives are usually placed after the noun!

Plural of adjectives

The following chart shows the plural of adjectives. Remember that you have to first find the stem before you can add the proper ending to the word.

skemmtilegur (fun)			
	Masculine	**Feminine**	**Neuter**
Singular	skemmtileg-*ur*	skemmtileg	skemmtileg-*t*
Plural	skemmtileg-*ir*	skemmtileg-*ar*	skemmtileg

Examples:

Hér eru rauðir vettlingar.	Here are red mittens.
Þarna eru þrjú græn epli.	Over there are three green apples.

Unstressed vowels may also disappear when you form the plural of adjectives:

gamal-*l* maður	old man
gaml-*ir* menn	old men

The verb combination *að fara að* + infinitive

The verb combination **að fara að** + *infinitive* is used to show that something is going to happen. It is the same as *to go to* or *to be just about to* in English.

Ég fer að sofa.	I am going to sleep.
Ég fer að fara.	I am just about to leave.

You can add intentionality to this construction by combining **að ætla að** with **að fara að** as in this sentence from the camping dialogue:

> **Gunnar og Hrafnhildur eru orðin mjög þreytt og ætla að fara að sofa.**
> Gunnar and Hrafnhildur are very tired and are going to go to sleep.

This construction is very common in Icelandic, even though it might sound a bit redundant.

Irregular verb: *að vilja* (to want)

The verb **vilja** *want* is irregular in the singular. It conjugates as follows:

að vilja (to want)

Person	Singular			Plural		
1ˢᵗ	**ég**	**vil**	I want	**við**	**vil-j-*um***	we want
2ⁿᵈ	**þú**	**vil-t**	you want	**þið**	**vil-j-*ið***	you want
3ʳᵈ *m.*	**hann**		he	**þeir**		
f.	**hún**	**vil-l**	she wants	**þær**	**vil-j-*a***	they want
neu.	**það**		it	**þau**		

Remember that the **double-l** in third person singular is pronounced with a *tl* sound just like in **sæll!**

> **Hrafnhildur vill fara**   Hrafnhildur wants to go camping.
> **í útilegu.**
> **Viltu fá þér eitthvað að borða?**   Would you like to have something to eat?

Æfingar – Exercises

1. **Find the definite plural for the following words:**

     Singular   **Plural indefinite**   **Plural definite**

     a.   stelpa   _____   _____

     b.   diskur   _____   _____

     c.   mynd   _____   _____

d. bók _____ _____

e. maður _____ _____

f. kona _____ _____

g. barn _____ _____

h. klukka _____ _____

i. köttur _____ _____

j. penni _____ _____

k. steinn _____ _____

l. borg _____ _____

2. **Change the following sentences to plural:**

a. Þetta er tölvan mín.

Þetta eru _____

b. Þetta er svartur hundur.

Þetta eru _____

c. Hér er grænn stóll.

Hér eru _____

d. Hér er skemmtilegur maður.

Hér eru _____

e. Hér er íslensk kona.

Hér eru _____

f. Þetta er sætt barn.

Hér eru _____

3. Translate the following into English:

a. Ég ætla að fara í bíó.

_____

b. Þú ætlar að fara að fara.

_____

c. Við ætlum að fara að sofa.

_____

d. Við förum að sofa.

_____

e. Við erum búin að vera að læra.

_____

LESSON 9

Ég sé hval!

◇◇◇◇◇◇

I see a whale!

Samtal 1: Ég sé hval!

Jeremy er á ferðalagi um Ísland. Hann er búinn að keyra um Norðurland í tvær vikur og nú er hann staddur á Húsavík. Á Húsavík hittir hann Steingrím. Steingrímur á bát og Jeremy fær strax áhuga á að fara með honum í siglingu. Þegar báturinn er kominn út á sjó verður Jeremy mjög sjóveikur. Honum líður ekki vel. Hann vill fara strax í land en Steingrímur er mjög spenntur og vill vera lengur.

Steingrímur:	Jeremy, ég sé hval! Komdu og sjáðu, þarna er hvalur!
Jeremy:	Æi, Steingrímur, ég er veikur. Ég vil bara vera í friði.
Steingrímur:	Þetta er frábært! Og þarna sé ég líka lunda! Vá, hvað hann er sætur!
Jeremy:	Ææ. Mér líður svo illa. Ég vil fara heim.
Steingrímur:	Og þarna er annar lundi. Sjórinn er mjög fallegur í dag. Hann er svo grænn! Hefur þú séð svona fallegan sjó?
Jeremy:	Æi.
Steingrímur:	Vá, og þarna sé ég líka regnboga. Sjáðu Jeremy, þarna er regnbogi!
Jeremy:	Steingrímur, hvað er klukkan? Hvenær komum við í land?
Steingrímur:	Klukkan er tvö. Við komum bráðum í land. Ó, ég er svo svangur. Ég ætla að borða þegar við komum. Ég ætla að kaupa mér hamborgara!
Jeremy:	Þegiðu Steingrímur! Hættu þessu!
Steingrímur:	Æi, fyrirgefðu Jeremy. Ég skal ekki tala um mat.

Samtal 2

Þegar Steingrímur og Jeremy koma í land fara þeir beint á veitingastað. Jeremy er ekki lengur sjóveikur og þeir eru báðir mjög svangir.

Þjónn:	Góðan dag, get ég aðstoðað ykkur?
Steingrímur:	Já, gæti ég fengið að sjá matseðil?
Þjónn:	Gjörðu svo vel.

Dialogue 1: I see a whale!

Jeremy is travelling around Iceland. He has been driving around north Iceland for two weeks, and he is now in Húsavík. In Húsavík he meets Steingrímur. Steingrímur has a boat, and Jeremy is immediately interested in going sailing with him. When the boat is out on the ocean, Jeremy becomes very seasick. He doesn't feel well. He wants to go immediately to shore, but Steingrímur is very excited and wants to stay longer.

Steingrímur:	Jeremy, I see a whale! Come and see, there is a whale over there!
Jeremy:	Oh Steingrímur, I'm sick. I just want to be left alone.
Steingrímur:	This is fantastic! And there I also see a puffin! Wow, he is cute!
Jeremy:	Oooh, I feel so bad. I want to go home.
Steingrímur:	And there is another puffin. The ocean is so beautiful today. It is so green. Have you ever seen such a beautiful ocean?
Jeremy:	Ohh.
Steingrímur:	Wow, and I also see a rainbow there. Look Jeremy, there is a rainbow!
Jeremy:	Steingrímur, what time is it? When do we get back to shore?
Steingrímur:	It's two o'clock. We will get back soon. Oh, I'm so hungry. I'm going to eat when we get back. I am going to buy myself a hamburger!
Jeremy:	Shush Steingrímur! Stop it!
Steingrímur:	Oh, sorry Jeremy. I will not talk about food.

Dialogue 2

When Steingrímur and Jeremy come to shore, they go straight to a restaurant. Jeremy is not seasick anymore, and they are both very hungry.

Waiter:	Hello, what can I do for you?
Steingrímur:	Yes, could I see a menu, please?
Waiter:	There you go.

Fimm mínútum síðar:

Þjónn:	Jæja, eruð þið tilbúnir að panta?
Steingrímur:	Já, ég ætla að fá hamborgara og franskar kartöflur.
Þjónn:	Já, og hvað má bjóða þér?
Jeremy:	Ég ætla að fá súpu dagsins og salat.
Þjónn:	Má bjóða ykkur eitthvað að drekka?
Jeremy:	Mig langar bara í vatn.
Steingrímur:	Og bjór fyrir mig, takk.

Five minutes later:

Waiter:	Are you ready to order?
Steingrímur:	Yes, I'm going to have a hamburger and french fries.
Waiter:	Yes, and what would you like to have?
Jeremy:	I'm going to have the soup of the day and salad.
Waiter:	May I offer you something to drink?
Jeremy:	I would just like some water, please.
Steingrímur:	And beer for me, thanks.

Orðaforði – Vocabulary

annar *adj. m.* another
áhugi *n. m.* interest
báðir *pron. m. pl.* both
bjór *n. m.* beer
fallegur *adj. m.* beautiful
ferðalag *n. neu.* journey, voyage
franskar kartöflur *n. f. pl.* french fries
í friði in peace
að geta *v3* to be able
grænn *adj. m.* green
gæti *v3 past subj., see* **að geta**
hamborgari *n. m.* hamburger
að hitta *v2* to meet
honum *pron. dat.* he *(to him)*
hvalur *n. m.* whale
hættu! *v2 imp.* stop!
að keyra *v2* to drive
að langa *v1* to want
lengur *adv.* longer
lundi *n. m.* puffin

matseðill *n. m.* menu
að panta *v1* to order
regnbogi *n. m.* rainbow
sé *v5, see* **að sjá**
sigling *n. f.* sailing
sjór *n. m.* ocean
spenntur *adj. m.* excited
staddur *adj. m.* located
sjóveikur *adj. m.* seasick
sjór *n. m.* ocean
að sjá *v5* to see
sjáðu! *v5 imp.* look!
súpa *n. f.* soup
sætur *adj. m.* cute, sweet
um *prep.* around, about
vatn *n. neu.* water
veikur *adj. m.* sick
veitingastaður *n. m.* restaurant
þegiðu! *v2 imp.* shush!
þjónn *n. m.* waiter

Orðasambönd – Useful expressions

Áttu borð fyrir einn? — Do you have a table for one?
  tvo? — two?
  þrjá? — three?
  fjóra ? — four?
  fimm? — five?

Gæti ég fengið að sjá matseðilinn? — Could I take a look at the menu?
Hver er réttur dagsins? — What is today's special?
Hver er súpa dagsins? — What is the soup of the day?

Er þetta borð frátekið? — Is this table reserved?
Er þessi stóll frátekinn? — Is this chair taken?

Ég ætla að fá ...	I'm going to have ...
súpu dagsins.	the soup of the day.
hamborgara.	a hamburger.
steik.	steak.
fisk dagsins.	today's fish
rétt dagsins.	today's special.
Gæti ég fengið reikninginn?	Could I have the check, please?

What are cases?

In case languages, verbs and prepositions can take specific cases. This means that certain verbs and prepositions will require their objects to be in a certain case.

In Icelandic, nouns, adjectives, pronouns, and some numerals have four different cases: nominative, accusative, dative, and genitive. So far, most of the nouns we have seen have been in the nominative case. The nominative is used when we refer to the subject of a sentence, or the person who is performing the action.

Consider the title of this lesson: **Ég sé hval** *I see a whale.* In this sentence, **ég** is the subject and **hvalur** is the object. I am the one looking, so *I* is the subject. The whale is the thing that is being seen, and thus is the object.

Nominative

Only a very few verbs take the nominative: **vera** *be*, **verða** *become*, **heita** *be called.*

Hún heitir *Anna.*	Her name is Anna.
Anna er *sálfræðingur.*	Anna is a psychologist.
Ég verð *kennari.*	I will become a teacher.

Most other verbs–and all prepositions–are followed by another case, either accusative, dative, or genitive. In this lesson we are going to focus on the accusative.

When to use the accusative

1. Direct object

The accusative is used to indicate the *direct object of a phrase*, or the person, thing, or idea that is affected or perceived by the subject. It is useful to ask the question *what?* to yourself after the verb to determine whether the object is direct and should be in the accusative case. In the example below, **Ég elska hann**, you can ask *I love what?* and answer *him*. Therefore, *him* is a direct object and should be in the accusative case. For now, we will focus on direct objects, but you should be aware that sometimes you cannot answer the question *what?* and so the object will be a different kind of object.

Ég elska *hann*.	I love *him*.
Gunnar borðar *appelsínu*.	Gunnar eats an *orange*.

2. Prepositions

Certain prepositions take the accusative case. The preposition **um** *about* is one of these prepositions.

Ég tala *um afa*.	I talk *about my grandfather*.
Bíómyndin er *um strák*.	The movie is *about a boy*.

The prepositions **í** and **á** are followed by accusative when they denote a movement to a place:

Ég fer *á veitingastað*.	I go *to a restaurant*.
Við förum bráðum *í land*.	We will soon go *ashore*.

3. Certain impersonal constructions

Certain verbs are known as impersonal verbs. The verbs **vanta** *need*, *lack*, **dreyma** *dream*, and **langa** *want* are such verbs. These verbs have no nominative subject. Instead, what would in English go in the nominative-subject position is put into the accusative case.

***Ara* vantar penna.**	*Ari* needs a pen.
***Hann* langar í pítsu.**	*He* wants pizza.
***Hana* dreymir um að læra íslensku.**	*She* dreams about learning Icelandic.

Strong nouns in the accusative

This table shows you what regular strong nouns look like in nominative and accusative singular.

	hval/ur (whale)	**mynd** (picture)	**barn** (child)
	Masculine	**Feminine**	**Neuter**
Nom.	hval-*ur*	mynd	barn
Acc.	hval	mynd	barn

Feminine and neuter are easy to learn, because they have no ending in nominative. The nominative is therefore exactly the same as the accusative.

Nominative		**Accusative**	
Hér er bók.	Here is a book.	**Ég les bók.**	I read a book.
Hér er blóm.	Here is a flower.	**Ég gef blóm.**	I give a flower.
Hér er kaffi.	Here is coffee.	**Ég drekk kaffi.**	I drink coffee.

When you form the accusative of masculine nouns, the endings **ur**, **r**, **l**, and **n** disappear.

Nominative		**Accusative**	
Hann er gest-*ur*.	He is a guest.	**Ég er með gest.**	I have a guest.
Hér er stein-*n*.	Here is a stone.	**Ég sé stein.**	I see a stone.
Hér er stól-*l*.	Here is a chair.	**Ég er með stól.**	I have a chair.
Þarna er sjó-*r*.	There is an ocean.	**Ég sé sjó.**	I see an ocean.

Weak nouns in the accusative

Weak nouns end in a vowel, and this vowel will often change to indicate case.

	pabb/i (dad)	**klukk/a** (clock)	**aug/a** (eye)
	Masculine	**Feminine**	**Neuter**
Nom.	pabb-*i*	klukk-*a*	aug-*a*
Acc.	pabb-*a*	klukk-*u*	aug-*a*

MASCULINE

Nominative		Accusative	
Þetta er bakpok-*i.*	This is a backpack.	**Ég á bakpok-*a.***	I have a backpack.
Þetta er Ól-*i.*	This is Óli.	**Ég tala við Ól-*a.***	I talk with Óli.

FEMININE

Nominative		Accusative	
Hér er píts-*a.*	Here is a pizza.	**Ég borða píts-*u.***	I eat a pizza.
Ég heiti Ev-*a.*	My name is Eva.	**Óli er giftur Ev-*u.***	Óli is married to Eva.

When a feminine noun has an **a** in the stem, such as in the word **k*a*ka**, the **u** sound in the accusative form causes a vowel shift in the stem. You might be starting to notice a pattern here in Icelandic! A **u** ending often results in the vowel **a** in the stem shifting to an **ö**. Notice, however, that it is only the last syllable before the **u** sound that is affected.

Nominative		Accusative	
Þetta er k*a*k-*a.*	This is a cake.	**Ég baka kök-*u.***	I bake a cake.
Þetta er *a*mm-*a.*	This is grandmother.	**Ég tala við ömm-*u.***	I talk to grandmother.

It is important to be able to identify the accusative in both masculine and feminine weak nouns and not to confuse the two. Sometimes it can be tricky. Consider the following examples:

Ég heiti Helg-*a.*	My name is Helg*a*.
Þetta er Helg-*i.*	This is Helg*i*.
Ég sé Helg-*a.*	I see Helg*i*.
Helg-*a* elskar Helg-*a.*	Helga loves Helg*i*.

Almost all names that end in an **a** sound in nominative are women's names. The only exception is the name **Sturl-*a***, which is a man's name but declines as a feminine noun: **Ég sé Sturl-*u*** *I see Sturla.*

Neuter words that end in **a** in the nominative have the same ending in the accusative.

NEUTER

Nominative		Accusative	
Hér er hjart-*a*.	Here is a heart.	**Þú ert með gott hjart-*a*.**	You have a good heart.
Þetta er Kanada.	This is Canada.	**Ég fer til Kanada.**	I go to Canada.

Plural nouns in the accusative

The accusative plural declines in the following way:

Nominative and Accusative Plural Noun Endings

	Masculine		Feminine		Neuter	
	strák/ar (boys) hval/ir (whales)		kon/ur (women) mynd/ir (images)		börn (children) aug/u (eyes)	
Nom.	strák-*ar*	hval-*ir*	kon-*ur*	mynd-*ir*	börn	aug-*u*
Acc.	strák-*a*	hval-*i*	kon-*ur*	mynd-*ir*	börn	aug-*u*

Ég sé hval*i*.	I see whales.
Ég á tvö börn.	I have two children.

Pronouns: *annar* (another) and *báðir* (both)

In addition to meaning *second* the word **annar** is also used as a pronoun meaning *another one* or *someone else*.

annar (second, another one, someone else)

Masculine	Feminine	Neuter
annar	önnur	annað

Hvað annað eigum við að kaupa?	What else should we buy?
Þú ert allt önnur manneskja!	You are a totally new person!
Hver annar ætlar að koma?	Who else is coming?

The pronoun **báðir** *both* declines in gender like an adjective. Remember that it is a plural word so it has the same endings as plural adjectives do. Note also the vowel shift in neuter in which **á** shifts to **æ**.

Masculine	báðir (both) Feminine	Neuter
báð-*ir*	báð-*ar*	bæð-*i*

Steingrímur og Jeremy
  eru *báðir* sjóveikir.
Anna og Hanna eru
  báðar sjóveikar.
	Both Steingrímur and Jeremy
	  are seasick.
	Both Anna and Hanna are
	  seasick.

Imperative

The imperative form of verbs is used when speakers are giving orders, such as in *go* or *stop it*! In Icelandic, verbs of the type 1 conjugation form the imperative by adding the ending **ðu**, which is a phonetically reduced **þú** *you*, after the infinitive. Remember that the final **a** is a part of the stem.

Infinitive		Imperative
að skrifa to write	→	**Skrifaðu!** Write!
að grilla to barbecue	→	**Grillaðu!** Barbecue!
að tala to speak	→	**Talaðu!** Speak!

Verbs of the other four categories all form the imperative by adding **ðu**, **du**, **tu**, **ddu**, or **u** to the stem. The **a** ending in these verbs is not a part of the stem. The following table shows the main rules for forming the imperative:

When the stem ends in	Ending	Example	
a vowel	**ðu**	**að sjá** to see →	**Sjáðu!** Look!
f, **g**, voiced **r**	**ðu**	**að heyra** to hear →	**Heyrðu!** Listen!
g, **l**, **m** or **n**	**du**	**að koma** to come →	**Komdu!** Come!
vowel + **ð**	**ddu**	**að greiða** to pay →	**Greiddu!** Pay!
p, **t**, **k**, unvoiced **r** and **s**	**tu**	**að geta** to guess →	**Gettu!** Guess!

The plural imperative is formed simply by using the second person plural of the verb. The verb is often followed by the plural pronoun **þið** *you*. In spoken interaction, the ending **i** replaces the pronoun: **sjáið þið** → **sjáiði**.

Infinitive		**2nd Person Plural**		**Imperative Plural**	
að skrifa	to write	**skrifið**	you write	**skrifið þið!** *or* **skrifiði!**	Write!
að fara	to go	**farið**	you go	**farið þið!** *or* **fariði!**	Go!

Demonstrative pronouns: *þessi* and *þetta* (this)

The demonstrative pronoun **þessi** *this* declines in gender and number.

þessi and **þetta** (this)

	Masculine	**Feminine**	**Neuter**
Singular	**þessi maður** this man	**þessi kona** this woman	**þetta barn** this child
Plural	**þessir menn** these men	**þessar konur** these women	**þessi börn** these children

Þessi kona heitir Hildur. This woman is called Hildur.
Þetta fólk er frá Íslandi. These people are from Iceland.
Þessir menn ætla að læra íslensku. These men are going to learn Icelandic.

In cases where the pronoun is not immediately followed by a subject, the neuter form is used.

Þetta er ég. This is I.
Þetta er mamma mín. This is my mom.
Hver er þetta? Who is this?

Æfingar – Exercises

1. Put the following words into the accusative form:

a. köttur ____________________
b. hnífur ____________________
c. Ameríkani ____________________
d. kennari ____________________
e. vindur ____________________
f. tölva ____________________
g. mappa ____________________

  h.   bók   _____

  i.   glas   _____

  j.   sjónvarp   _____

  k.   þjónn   _____

  l.   matur   _____

  m. veitingastaður   _____

  n.   bátur   _____

2. Fill in the blanks:

  a.   Ég kaupi _____ _____ og _____
       (tómatur, banani, ostur).

  b.   Mamma borðar ekki _____ (kjúklingur).

  c.   Ég tala við _____ _____ og _____
       (pabbi, afi, frændi).

  d.   Ég sé _____ (bíll).

  e.   Sagan er um _____ og _____
       (Íslendingur, Kanadamaður).

3. Translate the following sentences:

  a.   Jeremy is very hungry now. He goes to a restaurant. He orders
       pizza and soup.

       _____

       _____

  b.   Steingrímur is going to buy a car.

       _____

       _____

  c.   Jeremy is learning Icelandic. He also speaks English and German.

       _____

       _____

  d.   Sigga loves Siggi.

       _____

4. Form imperatives:

a. að fara → _____ ! Go (away)!
b. að borða → _____ matinn þinn! Eat your food!
c. að borga → _____ reikninginn! Pay the check!
d. að elda → _____ fyrir mig! Cook for me!
e. að tala → _____ við mig! Talk to me!
f. að segja → _____ mér allt! Tell me everything!
g. að kenna → _____ mér íslensku! Teach me Icelandic!

LESSON 10

Búðarferð

◇◇◇◇◇

Going to the store

Samtal 1: Búðarferð

Í dag er laugardagur. Klukkan er tvö og Hrafnhildur og Gunnar eru að fara í búð. Þau eru búin að bjóða Jeremy í mat í kvöld.

Gunnar:	Jæja, hvað eigum við að elda í kvöld?
Hrafnhildur:	Hvað segirðu um lambakjöt? Lambakjötið er alltaf mjög gott.
Gunnar:	Já, lambakjöt er æðislega gott en er ekki Jeremy grænmetisæta?
Hrafnhildur:	Jú, alveg rétt! Hann borðar ekki kjöt. En borðar hann fisk? Eða borðar hann bara grænmeti?
Gunnar:	Kannski er öruggara að elda bara grænmetispítsu í kvöld, þá verður ekkert vandamál. Honum finnst pítsa ábyggilega góð.
Hrafnhildur:	Góð hugmynd. Bökum pítsu! Hvað eigum við þá að kaupa? Hvað eigum við heima og hvað vantar okkur?
Gunnar:	Við eigum hveiti, olíu og ger.
Hrafnhildur:	En eigum við tómatsósu?
Gunnar:	Nei, okkur vantar tómatsósu og okkur vantar líka ost.
Hrafnhildur:	Já, við skulum þá kaupa tómatsósu, ost, lauk, eina rauða papriku, einn tómat og kannski eina dós af ananas.
Gunnar:	Ananas?
Hrafnhildur:	Já, ananas er svo góður á pítsu.
Gunnar:	Allt í lagi. En hvað eigum við að vera með í eftirrétt?
Hrafnhildur:	Búum til ostaköku, hún er alltaf vinsæl. Þú býrð til svo rosalega góða sítrónuostaköku!
Gunnar:	Æi, ég hef ekki tíma til að búa til ostaköku. Mig langar bara í ís. Hann er alltaf bestur.
Hrafnhildur:	Allt í lagi. En drífum okkur núna út í búð.
Gunnar:	Já, förum.

Dialogue 1: Going to the store

Today is Saturday. It is two o'clock and Hrafnhildur and Gunnar are going to the store. They have invited Jeremy over for dinner tonight.

Gunnar:	Well, what should we cook tonight?
Hrafnhildur:	What do you think about lamb? Lamb is always very good.
Gunnar:	Yes, lamb is just fantastic, but isn't Jeremy a vegetarian?
Hrafnhildur:	Yes, that's right! He doesn't eat meat. But does he eat fish? Or does he only eat vegetables?
Gunnar:	Maybe it's safer to just make a vegetarian pizza tonight, then we are not going to have any problems. He surely thinks pizza is good.
Hrafnhildur:	Good idea. Let's bake a pizza! What should we buy then? What do we need and what do we have at home?
Gunnar:	We have flour, oil, and yeast.
Hrafnhildur:	But do we have tomato sauce?
Gunnar:	No, we need tomato sauce, and we also need cheese.
Hrafnhildur:	Yes, let's buy tomato sauce, cheese, onion, one red bell pepper, one tomato, and maybe one can of pineapple.
Gunnar:	Pineapple?
Hrafnhildur:	Yes, pineapple is really good on pizza.
Gunnar:	All right. But what should we have as a dessert?
Hrafnhildur:	Let's make a cheesecake, that's always popular. You make such a wonderful lemon cheesecake!
Gunnar:	Oh, I don't have time to make cheesecake. I just want ice cream. That's always the best.
Hrafnhildur:	Okay. But let's go to the store now.
Gunnar:	Yes, let's go.

Samtal 2

Gunnar og Hrafnhildur eru nú búin að ná í allt sem þau ætla að kaupa.
Þau ganga að kassanum og setja vörurnar á búðarborðið.

Afgreiðslumaður:	Góðan daginn!
Hrafnhildur:	Góðan dag!
Afgreiðslumaður:	Var það eitthvað fleira?
Hrafnhildur:	Já, ég ætla að fá súkkulaði. Hvað kostar þetta þarna?
Afgreiðslumaður:	Þetta kostar hundrað fimmtíu og tvær krónur.
Hrafnhildur:	Já, ég ætla að fá það.
Afgreiðslumaður:	Og eitthvað fleira?
Hrafnhildur:	Nei takk, þetta er komið.
Afgreiðslumaður:	Viltu poka?
Hrafnhildur:	Já takk.
Afgreiðslumaður:	Það gera tvö þúsund fimm hundruð sextíu og þrjár krónur.
Hrafnhildur:	Tekurðu kort?
Afgreiðslumaður:	Nei, því miður, bara reiðufé.
Hrafnhildur:	Ekkert mál. Gjörðu svo vel. Hér eru þrjú þúsund krónur.
Afgreiðslumaður:	Takk. Og hér er afgangurinn, fjögur hundruð þrjátíu og sjö krónur, gjörðu svo vel!
Hrafnhildur:	Þakka þér fyrir!

Dialogue 2

Gunnar and Hrafnhildur have now gathered everything they intend to buy. They walk up to the cashier and put the groceries on the counter.

Cashier:	Good day!
Hrafnhildur:	Good day!
Cashier:	Is there something else you would like to have?
Hrafnhildur:	Yes, I would like to have a chocolate bar. How much is that one over there?
Cashier:	This costs one hundred and fifty-two kronas.
Hrafnhildur:	Yes, I would like to have that, please.
Cashier:	And something else?
Hrafnhildur:	No thanks, this is everything.
Cashier:	Would you like a plastic bag?
Hrafnhildur:	Yes please.
Cashier:	That makes two thousand, five hundred and sixty-three kronas.
Hrafnhildur:	Do you take credit cards?
Cashier:	No, unfortunately, just cash.
Hrafnhildur:	No problem. There you go. This is three thousand kronas.
Cashier:	Thank you. And here is the change, four hundred thirty-seven kronas, there you go!
Hrafnhildur:	Thanks!

Orðaforði – Vocabulary

af *prep.* of
ananas *n. m.* pineapple
ábyggilega *adv.* surely
bestur *adv. superl. m.* best
að bjóða *v3* (**ég býð**) to invite
búðarborð *n. neu.* counter
dós *n. f.* tin
drífum okkur (**að drífa okkur** *v3*) let's
    get going (to hurry up)
eftirréttur *n. m.* dessert
ein *num. f.* one
eina *num. f. acc.*, *see* **ein**
fiskur *n. m.* fish
ger *n. neu.* yeast
grænmeti *n. neu. sing.* vegetable
grænmetispítsa *n. f.* vegetarian pizza
grænmetisæta *n. f.* vegetarian
hveiti *n. neu.* flour
ís *n. m.* ice cream
kassi *n. m.* checkout, cash register
kjöt *n. neu.* meat
kort *n. neu.* card
að kosta *v1* to cost
lambakjöt *n. neu.* lamb (meat)

laukur *n. m.* onion
olía *n. f.* oil
ostakaka *n. f.* cheesecake
ostur *n. m.* cheese
pítsa *n. f.* pizza
plastpoki *n. m.* plastic bag
rauð *adj. f.* red
rauða *adj. f. acc.*, *see* **rauð**
reiðufé *n. neu.* cash
sítrónuostakaka *n. f.* lemon
    cheesecake
að taka *v3* (**ég tek**) to take
tekurðu *v3* *2nd pers.*, *see* **að taka**
tími *n. m.* time
tómatsósa *n. f.* ketchup, tomato sauce
tómatur *n. m.* tomato
vandamál *n. neu.* problem
vara *n. f. sing.* article, goods
vörurnar *n. f. pl. def.*, *see* **vara**
þá *adv.* then
æðislega *adv.* madly (awfully)
æðislega gott *adj.* awfully good
öruggara *adj. comp. neu.* safer

Orðasambönd – Useful expressions

Hvað kostar þetta?   How much is this?

Hvað kostar …?   How much is …?
  mjólk?   milk?
  skyr?   skyr?
  þessi peysa?   this sweater?
  þetta póstkort?   this postcard?
  þessi diskur?   this CD?

Asking a taxi driver:

Hvað kostar ...?	How much is it ...?
að fara í bæinn?	to go downtown?
að fara á flugvöllinn?	to go to the airport?
að fara á Hótel ...?	to go to Hotel ...?

Icelandic money

The Icelandic currency is called **króna**, or **krónur** in plural. The abbreviated form is **kr**. **Krón-a** ends in **a** and is a feminine noun. Therefore, when talking about **króna** quantities between 1 and 4, you use the feminine form of the number:

(a) Numbers of Money from 1–20

1 kr. = *ein* króna	11 kr. = ellefu krónur
2 kr. = *tvær* krónur	12 kr. = tólf krónur
3 kr. = *þrjár* krónur	13 kr. = þrettán krónur
4 kr. = *fjórar* krónur	14 kr. = fjórtán krónur
5 kr. = fimm krónur	15 kr. = fimmtán krónur

6 kr. = sex krónur	16 kr. = sextán krónur
7 kr. = sjö krónur	17 kr. = sautján krónur
8 kr. = átta krónur	18 kr. = átján krónur
9 kr. = níu krónur	19 kr. = nítján krónur
10 kr. = tíu krónur	20 kr. = tuttugu krónur

(b) Numbers of Money from 30–100

30 kr. = þrjátíu krónur	70 kr. = sjötíu krónur
40 kr. = fjörutíu krónur	80 kr. = áttatíu krónur
50 kr. = fimmtíu krónur	90 kr. = níutíu krónur
60 kr. = sextíu krónur	100 kr. = *(eitt)*hundrað krónur

The numbers between the tens are expressed with the help of the conjunction **og** *and*:

tuttugu og ein króna	21 kr.
tuttugu og tvær krónur	22 kr.

Note that for numbers such as 21, 31, 41, etc. **króna** is in singular because only **ein** modifies it grammatically.

(c) Numbers of money starting from one hundred

Hundrað *hundred* and **hundruð** *hundreds* are neuter nouns, and thus, counted in neuter:

100 kr. = eitt hundra*ð* **krónur**	**600 kr. = sex hundruð krónur**
200 kr. = tvö hundruð krónur	**700 kr. = sjö hundruð krónur**
300 kr. = þrjú hundruð krónur	**800 kr. = átta hundruð krónur**
400 kr. = fjögur hundruð krónur	**900 kr. = níu hundruð krónur**
500 kr. = fimm hundruð krónur	

Numbers from 100–1000 also use the conjunction **og** between the last two numbers. When the number ends with a 10, 20, 30, etc., the conjunction is placed between the hundreds and the tens:

131 kr. = eitt hundra*ð* **þrjátíu** *og ein* **króna***a*
469 kr. = fjögur hundr*uð* **sextíu** *og níu* **krón***ur*
620 kr. = Sex hundr*uð og* **tuttugu krón***ur*

(d) Numbers of money starting from one thousand

Þúsund *thousand* is also a neuter noun and is therefore also counted in neuter:

1.000 kr. = eitt þúsund krónur
2.000 kr. = tvö þúsund krónur
3.000 kr. = þrjú þúsund krónur
4.000 kr. = fjögur þúsund krónur
5.000 kr. = fimm þúsund krónur
6.000 kr. = sex þúsund krónur

1.254 kr. = eitt þúsund tvö hundruð fimmtíu og fjórar krónur
10.344 kr. = tíu þúsund þrjú hundruð fjörutíu og fjórar krónur

230.560 kr. = tvö hundruð og þrjátíu þúsund fimm hundruð
                      og sextíu krónur

Notice that the conjunction **og** is also used before the last digit before the noun **þúsund**. Thus, it occurs twice in numbers this high.

Icelanders, like other Europeans, put a period between every third digit and a comma for the decimal marker. This is the opposite system from the one that is used in North America:

1,000.00 = one thousand
1.000,00 = **eitt þúsund**

Years

Ég fæddist árið I was born in …

1967. **nítján hundruð sextíu og sjö.**
2006. **tvö þúsund og sex.**

Personal pronouns in the accusative

The following chart shows the accusative for personal pronouns:

Nominative & Accusative of Personal Pronouns

person	Singular			Plural			
	nom.		acc.		nom.		acc.	
1ˢᵗ	ég	I	mig	me	við	we	okkur	us
2ⁿᵈ	þú	you	þig	you	þið	you	ykkur	you
3ʳᵈ m.	hann	he	hann	him	þeir		þá	
f.	hún	she	hana	her	þær	they	þær	them
neu.	það	it	það	it	þau		þau	

Hann kyssir hana.	He kisses her.
Hann sér hann.	He sees him.
Þær sjá þá.	They *(f.)* see them *(m.)*.

Reflexive pronouns in the accusative

The reflexive pronoun is used when a third person subject, singular as well as plural, is doing something to itself.

Hann meiðir *sig.*	He hurts himself.
Stelpan meiðir *sig.*	The girl hurts herself.
Þau meiða *sig.*	They hurt themselves.

Remember that it is obligatory to use the reflexive when the object and the subject refer to the same thing or person. If you do not use the reflexive and use the accusative of the personal pronoun instead, the pronoun will refer to another, different third person.

Hún meiðir *sig*.	She hurts herself.
Hún meiðir *hana*.	She hurts her. (i.e. she hurts some other woman)

Adjectives in the accusative

Like nouns, adjectives also decline. Remember that adjectives always have the same gender, number, and case as the nouns they describe. The following chart shows the declension of adjectives in singular (plural is in the Grammar Summary on pp. 194–195):

rólegur (quiet)   **svartur** (black)

	Masculine	**Feminine**	**Neuter**
nom.	róleg-*ur* svart-*ur*	róleg svört	róleg-*t* svart
acc.	róleg-*an* svart-*an*	róleg-*a* svart-*a*	róleg-*t* svart

Examples:

Þetta er skemmtileg-*ur* strák-*ur*.	This is a fun guy.
Ég sé skemmtileg-*an* strák.	I see a fun guy.
Anna er skemmtileg.	Anna is fun.
Ég þekki skemmtileg-*a* stelp-*u*.	I know a fun girl.
Þetta er róleg-*t* barn.	This is a quiet baby.
Ég á mjög róleg-*t* barn.	I have a very quiet baby.

Remember that the accusative is formed from the masculine stem. Thus, the accusative for feminine adjectives such as **svört** black is **svarta** since only the stem is used and the **a** ending does not cause a vowel shift.

To express possession: *að eiga, hafa,* and *vera með*

There are three different ways of expressing possession: **að hafa** *to have*, **að eiga** *to own*, and **að vera með** *to be with*. The conjugation of the three verbs is shown in the charts below:

að hafa *v3* (to have)

Singular		Plural	
ég hef	I have	við höf-*um*	we have
þú hef-*ur*	you have	þið haf-*ið*	you have
hann/hún/það hef-*ur*	he/she/it has	þeir/þær/þau haf-*a*	they have

að eiga *v. irr* (to own)

Singular		Plural	
ég á	I own	við eig-*um*	we own
þú á-*tt*	you own	þið eig-*ið*	you own
hann/hún/það á	he/she/it owns	þeir/þær/þau eig-*a*	they own

að vera með *v. irr* (to be with)

Singular		Plural	
ég er með	I am with	við er-*um* með	we are with
þú er-*t* með	you are with	þið er-*uð* með	you are with
hann/hún/það er með	he/she/it is with	þeir/þær/þau er-*u* með	they are with

Remember that all these verbs are followed by an object, i.e. a noun or pronoun in the accusative.

Að hafa:

The verb **að hafa** *to have* is only used with abstract phenomena.

að hafa tíma	to have time
að hafa áhuga	to have interest

Að eiga:

The verb **að eiga** *to own* is used

a) for showing family relations:

að eiga foreldra	to have parents
að eiga systur	to have a sister
að eiga kærasta	to have a boyfriend

b)   when you want to emphasize ownership:

að eiga bíl	to own a car
að eiga íbúð	to own an apartment
að eiga pening	to own money
að eiga tölvu	to own a computer

Að vera með:

The construction **að vera með** *to be with* is used in the following contexts:

a)   when you are referring to accessories:

að vera með gleraugu	to have glasses
að vera með belti	to have a belt
að vera með húfu	to have a hat

b)   when you are referring to things that you have in your home or at your disposal, but you do not own them, or you do not necessarily want to emphasize your ownership:

að vera með mynd á veggnum	to have a picture on the wall
að vera með tölvu	to have a computer
að vera með bíl	to have a car
að vera með hund	to have a dog

c)   when you have something with you *now*:

að vera með pening	to have money *(with you now)*
að vera með bókina	to have the book *(with you now)*

Eiga að + infinitive

The verb **að eiga** does not always refer to possession as described in the section above. **Eiga** is sometimes followed by the infinitive marker **að** *to* and a verb in the infinitive. In these cases, the verb means that someone should do something or is supposed to do something.

Þú *átt að læra* íslensku.	You *are supposed to learn* Icelandic.
Ég *á að borða* grænmeti.	I'm *supposed to eat* vegetables.

You might think this sounds a bit like older English or a more formal language, and you'd be right! It's easy to remember **þú átt að** if you remember that it sounds like *you **ought** to!*

When this construction is used as an interrogative in first person plural, it means *should we?*

Eigum við að grilla?	Should we barbecue?
Eigum við að kaupa brauð?	Should we buy bread?

First person imperative: Let's ...

In English, to form the first person imperative you use the word *let's* and then add the infinitive of the verb: *Let's bake!*

In Icelandic, the construction is different. Icelandic simply uses the first person plural to form the imperative. The pronoun **við** *we* is not used; only the verb form is used in the imperative. Thus, **Bökum!** means *Let's bake!*

	person	**að baka** *v1* (to bake)	**að elda** *v1* (to cook)	**að grilla** *v1* (to barbecue)
Sing.	**1ˢᵗ**	bak-a	eld-a	grill-a
	2ⁿᵈ	bak-ar	eld-ar	grill-ar
	3ʳᵈ	bak-ar	eld-ar	grill-ar
Pl.	**1ˢᵗ**	*bök-um* (we) bake	*eld-um* (we) cook	*grill-um* (we) barbecue
	2ⁿᵈ	bak-*ið*	eld-*ið*	grill-*ið*
	3ʳᵈ	bak-*a*	eld-*a*	grill-*a*

Bökum!	Let's bake!
Eldum!	Let's cook!
Grillum!	Let's barbecue!

Notice the **u-shift** in first person plural in **baka**: the **a**-sound shifts to **ö** because of the **u**-sound in the ending, and this remains in the imperative form.

Æfingar – Exercises

1. **Translate the following sentences into Icelandic.**

   a. Dad buys a tomato and cheese.

   _____

   b. We bake a cake.

   _____

   c. Let's bake a cake!

   _____

   d. Guðlaugur loves Anna.

   _____

   e. Anna loves Árni.

   _____

   f. I see Helga, Hanna, Nonni, and Maggi.

   _____

   g. Grandpa bakes a pizza.

   _____

   h. Let's barbecue tonight!

   _____

   i. I'm a vegetarian. I eat only vegetables.

   _____

   j. What should we cook tonight?

   _____

2. **Fill in the blanks with the verbs *að eiga*, *að hafa*, or *að vera með*:**

   a. Ég _____ tvær systur. Þær heita Nanna og Laufey.
   b. Pabbi _____ ekki tíma til að tala við mig núna.
   c. Hver _____ þennan penna?
   d. Ég _____ ekki bíl, þess vegna fer ég alltaf með strætó.
   e. Anna _____ litla svarta kisu.
   f. Ari _____ ekki bíl sjálfur.

3. **Fill in the blanks with adjectives. Note that you first have to find the gender of the noun as all the adjectives are listed in masculine.**

   a. Jóhannes á _____ og _____ bíl. *(rauður, finn)*
   b. Ég á tvær fallegar peysur. Ég á eina _____ og eina _____
      _____. *(blár, hvítur)*
   c. Mamma kaupir _____ og _____ te. *(grænn,*
      svartur)
   d. Bróðir minn hlustar á mjög _____ tónlist! *(leiðinlegur)*

4. **Write the following numbers.**

   Ár:
   a. 1972 _____
   b. 1987 _____
   c. 2012 _____
   d. 1949 _____

   Krónur:
   e. 1.267,00 _____ krónur
   f. 150,00 _____ krónur
   g. 550,00 _____ krónur
   h. 2.371,00 _____ króna

   Dollarar:
   i. 20,00 _____ dollarar
   j. 12,00 _____ dollarar
   k. 4,00 _____ dollarar
   l. 142,00 _____ dollarar

LESSON 11

Í atvinnuviðtali

◇◇◇◇◇◇

In a job interview

Samtal: Í atvinnuviðtali

Jeremy er blankur og nú er hann að leita sér að vinnu. Hann sér
auglýsingu í glugga á geisladiskabúð þar sem stendur:

Starfsmaður óskast!

Við erum að leita að hressum, jákvæðum og hjálpsömum einstaklingi
með mikinn áhuga á tónlist. Verður að geta hafið störf sem fyrst.

Vinsamlegast hafið samband í síma 556 3453

Jeremy hringir í númerið og Jón svarar.

Jón:	Halló.
Jeremy:	Já, góðan daginn. Ég heiti Jeremy og ég er að leita mér að vinnu.
Jón:	Já, sæll. Þú hefur þá séð auglýsinguna mína.
Jeremy:	Já, og ég hef mikinn áhuga á að vinna í geisladiskabúð.
Jón:	Segðu mér fyrst aðeins frá sjálfum þér.
Jeremy:	Já, ég heiti sem sagt Jeremy og ég er frá Bandaríkjunum. Ég er að læra íslensku og þess vegna bý ég núna á Íslandi.
Jón:	Ég heyri að þú talar mjög góða íslensku en talarðu einhver önnur tungumál?
Jeremy:	Jú, móðurmálið mitt er enska og svo tala ég ágætis þýsku. Ég bjó í tvö ár í Þýskalandi.
Jón:	Já, svo þú talar bæði ensku og þýsku?
Jeremy:	Einmitt.
Jón:	Hvernig manneskja ertu?
Jeremy:	Ég er oftast glaðlyndur og jákvæður.
Jón:	En ertu hjálpsamur?
Jeremy:	Já, mér finnst mjög gaman að hjálpa fólki.
Jón:	Frábært, en hver eru áhugamál þín?

Dialogue: In a job interview

Jeremy is broke and now he is looking for a job. He sees an ad in a CD store window which says:

Employee wanted!

We are looking for a lively, positive, and helpful individual who has a big interest in music. Has to be able to start as soon as possible.

Please call 556 3453

Jeremy calls the number and Jón picks up the phone.

Jón: Hello.

Jeremy: Yes, hello. My name is Jeremy and I'm looking for a job.

Jón: Yes, hello. You must have seen my ad then.

Jeremy: Yes, and I'm very interested in working in a CD store.

Jón: First, tell me a bit about yourself.

Jeremy: Yes, as I said, my name is Jeremy, and I'm from the United States. I'm studying Icelandic and that's why I'm living in Iceland now.

Jón: I can tell that you speak very good Icelandic and do you speak any other languages?

Jeremy: Yes, my native language is English, and then I also speak German well. I lived in Germany for two years.

Jón: So you speak both English and German?

Jeremy: Exactly.

Jón: What kind of person are you?

Jeremy: I'm usually happy and positive.

Jón: Are you helpful?

Jeremy: Yes, I really enjoy helping people.

Jón: Great, and what are your interests?

Jeremy: Hmm, þetta er erfið spurning. Ég hef mikinn áhuga á
            tónlist. Ég hlusta til dæmis mjög mikið á rokk og ég hef
            sérstaklega mikinn áhuga á þungarokki og tölvutónlist.
            Svo hef ég náttúrulega áhuga á íþróttum. Ég hef áhuga á
            fótbolta, golfi, íshokkíi og sundi. Svo hef ég líka gaman af
            bókmenntum, bæði skáldsögum og ljóðum.

Jón: Þetta hljómar mjög vel. Ertu laus á morgun?

Jeremy: Hmm, this is a difficult question. I'm very interested in music. For example, I listen to rock a lot, and I'm especially interested in heavy metal and electronic music. And then I'm of course interested in sports. I'm interested in soccer, golf, ice hockey, and swimming. And I also enjoy literature, both novels and poems.

Jón: This sounds great. Are you available tomorrow?

Orðaforði – Vocabulary

á morgun tomorrow
ágætis *adj.* fine, very good
áhugamál *n. neu.* interest, hobby
bæði ... og *conj.* both ... and
auglýsing *n. f.* advertisement
áhugi *n. m.* interest
bjó *v5 past t., see* **búa**
blankur *adj. m.* broke
bókmenntir *n. f. pl.* literature
að búa *v5* (**ég bý**) to live
einstaklingur *n. m.* individual
fólk *n. neu.* people
fótbolti *n. m.* soccer
geisladiskabúð *n. f.* CD store
að geta *v3* to be able
glaðlyndur *adj. m.* happy *(type of person)*
gluggi *n. m.* window
golf *n. neu.* golf
hafið *v3, see* **hefja**
að hefja *v3* (**ég hef**) to start
að hjálpa *v1* to help
hjálpsamur *adj. m.* helpful
að hljóma *v1* to sound
að hlusta *v1* to listen
hress *adj. m.* lively, in good spirits
að hringja *v2* to call
íshokkí *n. neu.* ice hockey
íþrótt *n. f.* sport
jákvæður *adj. m.* positive, constructive
laus *adj. m.* available

að leita *v1* to seek
ljóð *n. neu.* poem
mikinn *adj. m.* great
móðurmál *n. neu.* mother tongue
óskast *v1 st-form* wanted
rokk *n. neu.* rock *(music)*
samband *n. neu.* contact
segðu *v2 imp.* tell
sem fyrst as soon as possible
sem sagt that is, as I said
séð *v5, see* **að sjá**
sérstaklega *adv.* especially
sími *n. m.* telephone
að sjá *v5* (**ég sé**) to see
sjálfur *pron. m.* self
skáldsaga *n. f.* novel
spurning *n. f.* question
að standa *v3* (**ég stend**) *here:* to be written
starfsmaður *n. m.* employee
störf *n. neu. pl., see* **starf**
starf *n. neu.* job
sund *n. neu.* swimming
að svara *v1* to answer
tónlist *n. f.* music
tungumál *n. neu.* language
tölvutónlist *n. f.* electronic music
vinsamlegast *adv. super.* kindly
Þýskaland *n. neu.* Germany
þungarokk *n. neu.* heavy metal

Orðasambönd – Useful expressions

Hver eru áhugamál þín?
Ég hef áhuga á ...
   íþróttum.
   tónlist.
   skák.
   listum.

What are your interests?
I'm interested in ...
   sports.
   music.
   chess.
   arts.

sögu.	history.
garðyrkju.	gardening.
ferðalögum.	travel.
fornmunum.	antiques.
fótbolta.	soccer.
Íslandi.	Iceland.
þjóðsögum.	folktales.
Íslendingasögunum.	the Icelandic sagas.
klassískri tónlist.	classical music.
píanóleik.	playing the piano.
útivist.	outdoor activities.
fjallgöngu.	mountain climbing.

How to use the dative

1. Indirect objects

If you recall when we learned the accusative, the accusative case was used when we could answer *what?* after the verb. In the sentence *I give him a book*, you can say *I give what?* and answer *a book*. Thus, the direct object is *a book*, and in Icelandic this is in the accusative case. However, you cannot ask *I give what?* and answer *him*—this simply doesn't make sense. We say that *him* is the indirect object. In Icelandic, you use the dative case to indicate an indirect object. Thus, whenever you can rephrase a sentence to include the phrase *to something or someone*, you use dative for the *something or someone* (see also Lesson 12).

að gefa *einhverjum* eitthvað	to give *someone* something
að lána *einhverjum* eitthvað	to lend *someone* something
að rétta *einhverjum* eitthvað	to hand *someone* something

2. With certain verbs

As mentioned in Lesson 9, most transitive verbs are followed by nouns in the accusative. There are, however, a few verbs that are always followed by objects in the dative.

að hjálpa	to help
að mæta	to meet *(e.g. on the street)*
að gleyma	to forget
að þakka	to thank

Examples:

Anna hjálpar _mömmu_.	Anna helps _mom_.
Ég gleymi _þér_ aldrei.	I will never forget _you_.
Þakka _þér_ kærlega fyrir!	Thanks a lot!

3. Impersonal constructions

Some constructions are considered impersonal. To understand this, think about certain actions as happening _to_ the experiencer rather than thinking about the experiencer doing the experiencing. An idea such as _I feel cold_ is expressed in Icelandic using the dative case: **mér er kalt**. Literally, this means _to me it is cold_. There is no nominative subject, so the construction seems strange to English speakers, but it is grammatically correct and complete in Icelandic.

You will have to learn which verbs create impersonal constructions, but a lot of them have to do with feeling and experiencing. The most common is **mér finnst** _I find_, as in the construction **mér finnst kalt hérna** _I find it cold here_.

Mér **finnst gaman að læra íslensku.**	I enjoy learning Icelandic.
Honum **finnst leiðinlegt að lesa.**	He finds it boring to read.
Okkur **sýnist þetta vera búið.**	It seems to us this is over.
Mér **er heitt.**	I feel hot.

You will notice that adjectives used in impersonal constructions are in neuter since they are not modifying any nominative subject. If you think about our literal translation above, _to me it is cold_, you can see how _cold_ does not directly describe _me_. Rather, the cold is happening _to me_. Thus, the adjective **kalt** is always in neuter singular, regardless of the gender and number of the people who are experiencing the cold.

Hildi er kalt.	Hildur feels cold.
Gunnari er kalt.	Gunnar feels cold.
Hrafnhildi og Gunnari er kalt.	Hrafnhildur and Gunnar are cold.

4. With certain prepositions

Some prepositions are always followed by objects in the dative:

frá	from
af	of
hjá	at, with, beside

úr	out of
við hliðina á	beside

Examples:

Ég er *frá* **Ísland***i*.	I'm from Iceland.
Jeremy er *frá* **Bandarík***junum*.	Jeremy is from the United States.
Ég er *úr* **sveit**.	I'm from the country.
Mamma er *hjá mér*.	Mom is with/beside me.
Hún situr *við hliðina á mér*.	She sits beside me.

The prepositions **í** *in* and **á** *on* are followed by objects in the dative if they signify a location and do not involve a movement to a place.

Ég er *í* **sturt***u*.	I am in the shower.
Mamma er *á* **Ísland***i*.	Mom is in Iceland.

Strong nouns in the dative

The inflectional ending for dative is added to the stem of the noun. The endings for strong nouns in singular are as follows:

Case Endings for Singular Strong Nouns

	Masculine hund/ur (dog) dal/ur (valley)		**Feminine** mynd (picture)	**Neuter** barn (child)
nom. sing.	hund-*ur*	dal-*ur*	mynd–	barn–
acc. sing.	hund–	dal–	mynd–	barn–
dat. sing.	hund-*i*	dal–	mynd–	barn-*i*

Note that the masculine dative may sometimes end in **i**. Unfortunately, there is no definite way to tell when to add an **i** and when not to. You will simply have to learn this on a case-by-case basis. The noun **hundur** is **hundi** in dative, but the noun **dalur** is simply **dal**. It can be helpful to use the number of consonants after the stem vowel to help you guess whether the noun should end with an **i** or not. Masculine nouns that have two consonants after the stem vowel tend to add an **i**, such as in **hund-ur** (the stem ends in **nd**). In **dalur** there is only one **l**, and therefore there is no **i** in the dative form. Of course, this rule does not work all the time, but it can help direct you when deciding whether to add an **i** or not.

Weak nouns in the dative

The dative for weak nouns is easy to memorize because it is exactly the same as the accusative:

Case Endings for Singular Weak Nouns

	Masculine pabb/i (dad)	Feminine klukk/a (clock)	Neuter aug/a (eye)
nom. pl.	pabb-*i*	klukk-*a*	aug-*a*
acc. pl.	pabb-*a*	klukk-*u*	aug-*a*
dat. pl.	pabb-*a*	klukk-*u*	aug-*a*

Plural nouns in the dative

The dative plural is easy because the three genders, both weak and strong, have the exact same ending. You simply have to add **um** to the stem!

Case Endings for Strong & Weak Plural Nouns

	Masculine strák/ar (boys)	Feminine kon/ur (women)	Neuter börn (children)
nom. plural	strák-*ar*	kon-*ur*	börn–
acc. plural	strák-*a*	kon-*ur*	börn–
dat. plural	strák-*um*	kon-*um*	börn-*um*

Examples:

Ég á fullt af vin-*um*.	I have a lot of friends.
Hér er alltof mikið af geisladisk-*um*!	There are too many CDs here!

Personal pronouns in the dative

Nominative & Dative of Personal Pronouns

person	Singular		Plural	
	nom.	**dat.**	**nom.**	**dat.**
1ˢᵗ	**ég** I	**mér** me	**við** we	**okkur** us
2ⁿᵈ	**þú** you	**þér** you	**þið** you	**ykkur** you
3ʳᵈ m.	**hann** he	**honum** him	**þeir**	
f.	**hún** she	**henni** her	**þær** they	**þeim** them
neu.	**það** it	**því** it	**þau**	

Examples:

Ég skal hjálpa þér.	I will help you.
Þú gleymir þeim alltaf!	You always forget them!

Reflexive pronouns in the dative

The dative of the reflexive pronoun is used when someone is doing something to or for himself or herself.

Jeremy er að leita *sér* að vinnu.	Jeremy is looking for a job *(for himself)*.

Adjectives in the dative

Adjectives also have a dative form. The following chart gives the various case endings for adjectives.

skemmtileg/ur (fun, interesting)

	Masculine	Feminine	Neuter
nom. sing.	skemmtileg-*ur*	skemmtileg	skemmtileg-*t*
acc. sing.	skemmtileg-*an*	skemmtileg-*a*	skemmtileg-*t*
dat. sing.	skemmtileg-*um*	skemmtileg-*ri*	skemmtileg-*u*

Ég gleymi aldrei skemmtileg-*u* fólki.	I never forget fun people.
Jeremy hefur áhuga á íslensk-*ri* tónlist.	Jeremy is interested in Icelandic music.

When an adjective stem ends in a vowel, such as **blá-r** *blue*, the r is doubled in the feminine dative.

blá/r (blue)

	Masculine	Feminine	Neuter
nom. sing.	blá-*r*	blá	blá-*tt*
acc. sing.	blá-*an*	blá-*a*	blá-*tt*
dat. sing.	blá-*um*	blá-*rri*	blá-*u*

When adjectives end in **n** or **l**, such as in **gamal-l** *old* or **feimin-n** *shy*, the stem endings and the inflectional endings in dative assimilate and become **ll** and **nn**.

gamal/l (old) and **fín/n** (neat)

	Masculine		Feminine		Neuter	
nom. sing.	gamal-*l*	fín-*n*	gömul	fín	gamal-*t*	fín-*t*
acc. sing.	gaml-*an*	fín-*an*	gaml-*a*	fín-*a*	gamal-*t*	fín-*t*
dat. sing.	göml-*um*	fín-*um*	gamal-*li*	fín-*ni*	göml-*u*	fín-*u*

In plural, adjectives decline in the following way:

skemmtileg/ur (fun, interesting)

	Masculine	Feminine	Neuter
nom. pl.	skemmtileg-*ir*	skemmtileg-*ar*	skemmtileg
acc. pl.	skemmtileg-*a*	skemmtileg-*ar*	skemmtileg
dat. pl.		skemmtileg-*um*	

Hér er fullt af skemmtileg*um* listamönnum.

There are lots of interesting artists here.

Æfingar – Exercises

1. **Find the dative for the following nouns:**

     a. bók   _____

     b. kisa   _____

     c. amma   _____

     d. bátur   _____

     e. hvalur   _____

     f. herbergi   _____

     g. stofa   _____

     h. tölva   _____

     i. klukka   _____

     j. matur   _____

     k. glas   _____

     l. rauðvín   _____

     m. smjör   _____

2. **Put the personal pronouns in dative:**

    a. Hver ætlar að hjálpa _____? (ég)
    b. Okkur langar að hjálpa _____ (þið)
    c. Ekki gleyma _____ (þau)
    d. Hver er hjá _____? (hún)
    e. Ég bý með _____ (hann)
    f. Ertu að leita að _____ (ég)

3. **Translate the following sentences:**

This is Árný. She lives in Iceland now, but she lived in England for three years. She speaks English very well. Árný works in a school. Árný is a very positive and lively person. She is very interested in sports, especially soccer and golf.

_____

_____

_____

_____

_____

_____

LESSON 12

Að kaupa afmælisgjafir

◇◇◇◇◇◇

Buying birthday gifts

Samtal: Að kaupa afmælisgjafir

Gunnar:	Heyrðu, Hrafnhildur, á morgun er tuttugasti og níundi júlí. Á ekki pabbi þinn afmæli þá?
Hrafnhildur:	Jú, það er rétt! Hann á afmæli á morgun. Við verðum að kaupa handa honum afmælisgjöf.
Gunnar:	Já, hvað eigum við að gefa honum? Eigum við að kaupa geisladisk?
Hrafnhildur:	Æi, mér finnst svo erfitt að gefa pabba mínum geisladiska. Hann hlustar bara á djass og mér finnst djass svo leiðinlegur. Ég vil frekar kaupa handa honum peysu eða skyrtu. Hann vantar alltaf föt.
Gunnar:	Æi, ég vil ekki gefa honum föt. Þú mátt gefa honum peysu ef ég má gefa honum disk. Ég veit að hann hefur svo gaman af tónlist og ég er búinn að ákveða hvaða disk ég ætla að kaupa handa honum.
Hrafnhildur:	Allt í lagi. En svo megum við ekki gleyma því að Jeremy á afmæli fyrsta ágúst. Hann er búinn að bjóða okkur í afmælisveislu.
Gunnar:	Nú er það? Frábært. Er það núna á föstudaginn?
Hrafnhildur:	Nei, það er á laugardaginn.
Gunnar:	Nú já. Hvað eigum við að gefa honum? Er kannski nóg að koma með blóm?
Hrafnhildur:	Nei, eigum við ekki að kaupa eitthvað fallegt handa honum?
Gunnar:	Ég veit! Gefum honum íslenska orðabók. Ég er alltaf að lána honum orðabókina mína.
Hrafnhildur:	Allt í lagi. Það er góð hugmynd.
Gunnar:	Þetta verður dýr mánuður. Við þurfum að kaupa peysu og geisladisk handa pabba þínum, og orðabók og blóm handa Jeremy.
Hrafnhildur:	Já, kannski sleppum við því bara að kaupa blóm handa Jeremy.
Gunnar:	Allt í lagi, og við kannski sleppum því þá líka að kaupa peysu handa pabba þínum. Það er nóg að gefa honum geisladisk.
Hrafnhildur:	Jæja, allt í lagi. Segjum það þá.
Gunnar:	Drífum okkur þá í búðina!

Dialogue: Buying birthday gifts

Gunnar:	Listen, Hrafnhildur, tomorrow is the twenty-ninth of July. Isn't that your dad's birthday?
Hrafnhildur:	Yes, that's right! His birthday is tomorrow. We have to buy a birthday present for him.
Gunnar:	Yes, what should we get for him? Should we buy him a CD?
Hrafnhildur:	Ah, it's so difficult to give CDs to dad. He only listens to jazz, and I find jazz so boring. I would rather want to get him a sweater or a shirt. He always needs clothes.
Gunnar:	Oh, I don't want to give him clothes. You can give him a sweater if I can give him a CD. I know that he likes music so much, and I have already decided which CD I'm going to get for him.
Hrafnhildur:	All right. But then we can't forget that August first is Jeremy's birthday. He has invited us to a party.
Gunnar:	Oh really? Great. Is that on Friday?
Hrafnhildur:	No, it's Saturday.
Gunnar:	Oh, okay. What should we give him? Is it maybe enough to bring flowers?
Hrafnhildur:	No, shouldn't we buy something nice for him?
Gunnar:	I know! Let's give him an Icelandic dictionary. I'm always lending him my dictionary.
Hrafnhildur:	Okay. That's a good idea.
Gunnar:	This is going to be an expensive month. We have to buy a sweater and a CD for your dad, and a dictionary and flowers for Jeremy.
Hrafnhildur:	Yes, maybe we will just skip buying flowers for Jeremy.
Gunnar:	Okay, and maybe then we should also skip buying a sweater for your dad. It's enough to give him a CD.
Hrafnhildur:	Yes, that's right. Okay, let's do that.
Gunnar:	Let's go to the store then!

Orðaforði – Vocabulary

afmæli *n. neu.* birthday
afmælisgjöf *n. f.* birthday present
afmælisveisla *n. f.* birthday party
blóm *n. neu.* flower
djass *n. m.* jazz
dýr *adj. m.* expensive
erfitt *adj. neu.* difficult
frekar *adv.* rather
geisladiskur *n. m.* CD
að hlusta *v1* to listen
hugmynd *n. f.* idea

að kaupa *v2* to buy
að lána *v1* to lend
leiðinlegur *adj. m.* boring
mátt *v.,* see **að mega**
að mega *v. irr.* may
nóg *adv.* enough
orðabók *n. f.* dictionary
peysa *n. f.* sweater
skyrta *n. f.* shirt, blouse
að sleppa *v2* to skip
að þurfa *v. irr.* to need

Dates

When you are referring to dates in Icelandic, use the masculine form of ordinal numbers:

fyrsti	first	**tólfti**	twelfth
annar	second	**þrettándi**	thirteenth
þriðji	third	**fjórtándi**	fourteenth
fjórði	fourth	**fimmtándi**	fifteenth
fimmti	fifth	**sextándi**	sixteenth
sjötti	sixth	**sautjándi**	seventeenth
sjöundi	seventh	**átjándi**	eighteenth
áttundi	eighth	**nítjándi**	nineteenth
níundi	ninth	**tuttugasti**	twentieth
tíundi	tenth	**þrítugasti**	thirtieth
ellefti	eleventh	**þrítugasti og fyrsti**	thirty-first

Names of months are not capitalized in Icelandic. The names are as follows:

janúar	January	**júlí**	July
febrúar	February	**ágúst**	August
mars	March	**september**	September
apríl	April	**október**	October
maí	May	**nóvember**	November
júní	June	**desember**	December

The months take the preposition **í**:

Ég á afmæli í mars. My birthday is in March.
Mamma á afmæli í nóvember. Mom's birthday is in November.

Note that when you are saying that something happened or will happen on a certain date, you have to put the ordinal number in the accusative. Thus, the proper form is:

Í dag er fimmt-*i* mars. Today is March fifth. *(nominative)*

but

Ég á afmæli fimmt-*a* mars. My birthday is *(on)* March fifth. *(accusative)*

Icelanders write dates in the format day/month rather than month/day. Thus, 5/4 means April fifth, not May fourth.

To give someone something

When you want to say that someone is giving something to someone, you have to use three different cases: nominative, accusative, and dative. The person who is giving is in the nominative, the person who is receiving is in the dative, and the thing that is being given is in the accusative.

---

giver (*nom.*) + VERB + receiver (*dat.*) + object (*acc.*)

Ég gef þér blóm. I give you a flower.
Kærastan mín gefur mér hring. My girlfriend gives me a ring.
Afi gefur ömmu súkkulaði. Grandfather gives grandmother chocolate.

Gefa is not the only verb that uses this construction. Instead of **gefa** you can use the verbs **senda** *send*, **lána** *lend*, **rétta** *hand*, **kenna** *teach*, and **segja** *tell*.

Gunnar lánar mér bók. Gunnar lends me a book.
Amma segir mér sögu. Grandma tells me a story.
Viltu rétta mér saltið? Could you hand me the salt?
María kennir honum íslensku. María teaches him Icelandic.

To buy something for someone

The verb **kaupa** *buy* has a slightly different structure. In this construction, you use the preposition **handa** before the receiver.

---

buyer (*nom.*) + **kaupa** + object (*acc.*) + **handa** + receiver (*dat.*)

Ég kaupi mynd handa þér.	I buy a picture for you.
Gunnar kaupir disk handa pabba.	Gunnar buys a CD for dad.

Possessive pronouns in the dative

This chart shows possessive pronouns **minn** (my, mine) and **þinn** (your, yours) in the dative. When the object in the dative requires a possessive, the possessive pronoun is also in the dative.

Singular of Possessive Pronouns
minn (my, mine) and þinn (your, yours)

	Masculine	Feminine	Neuter
Nom.	minn/þinn	mín/þín	mitt/þitt
Acc.	minn/þinn	mín-*a*/þín-*a*	mitt/þitt
Dat.	mín-*um*/þín-*um*	minn-*i*/þinn-*i*	mín-*u*/þín-*u*

Ég kaupi blóm handa pabba *mínum*.	I buy flowers for my dad.
Ég sendi mömmu *þinni* bréf.	I send a letter to your mother.

Plural of Possessive Pronouns
minn (my, mine) and þinn (your, yours)

	Masculine	Feminine	Neuter
Nom.	mín-*ir*/þín-*ir*	mín-*ar*/þín-*ar*	mín/þín
Acc.	mín-*a*/þín-*a*	mín-*ar*/þín-*ar*	mín/þín
Dat.	mín-*um*/þín-*um*		

Ég kaupi blóm handa foreldrum mínum.	I buy flowers for my parents.

Æfingar – Exercises

1. Write sentences using the following words:

    a. Bróðir minn + lána + mamma + bíll

___

    b. Ég + rétta + þú + salt og pipar

___

    c. Amma + senda + ég + pakki

___

    d. Kærastinn minn + gefa + ég + kettlingur

___

    e. Hrafnhildur + kaupa + gjöf + Gunnar

___

    f. Kennarinn + segja + ég + saga

___

    g. Jeremy + senda + við + póstkort

___

    h. Mamma + kaupa + penni, blýantur og skólataska + ég

___

    i. Ég + gefa + pabbi og mamma + hundur

___

2. Write the dates in the proper form:

    a. Í dag er   _____ (6/11)
    b. Ég á afmæli   _____ (4/3)
    c. Pabbi minn á afmæli   _____ (23/8)
    d. Ég fer til Íslands   _____ (21/5)
    e. Ég fer heim   _____ (30/5)
    f. Á morgun er   _____ (24/12)

LESSON 13

Hvar er farsíminn minn?

◇◇◇◇◇◇

Where is my cell phone?

Samtal: Hvar er farsíminn minn?

Hrafnhildur:	Gunnar, hvar er farsíminn minn?
Gunnar:	Er hann ekki í eldhúsinu? Ég sá símann á eldhúsborðinu.
Hrafnhildur:	Nei, hann er ekki þar. Ég er búin að leita alls staðar. Ég er meira að segja búin að leita í ísskápnum og undir vaskinum.
Gunnar:	En ertu búin að skoða í stofunni eða í svefnherberginu?
Hrafnhildur:	Já, ég er búin að skoða alls staðar í íbúðinni.
Gunnar:	Gleymdir þú honum í vinnunni þinni? Þú gleymir símanum þínum mjög oft á skrifborðinu þínu. Þú ert svo gleymin!
Hrafnhildur:	Ég? Ég er sko alls ekkert gleymin! Það ert þú sem gleymir alltaf öllu. Manstu þegar þú týndir kreditkortinu þínu í bænum og við þurftum að leita og leita í marga klukkutíma?
Gunnar:	Já, það var ég, en það var bara einu sinni. Þú týnir einhverju á hverjum degi. Ég er alltaf að hjálpa þér að finna lyklana þína, símann þinn, töskuna þína, veskið þitt og meira að segja gleraugun þín. Hvenær heldurðu að þú týnir sjálfri þér?
Hrafnhildur:	Æi, hættu að gera grín að mér. Þú veist að ég er mjög viðkvæm.
Gunnar:	Já, fyrirgefðu. Þú veist af mér finnst bara gaman að grínast í þér.
Hrafnhildur:	Kannski er síminn bara í vinnunni, annað hvort á skrifborðinu mínu eða á kaffistofunni. Ég var að tala í farsímann minn í dag áður en ég fór þaðan. Ég er eiginlega viss um að hann sé þar.
Gunnar:	Já, af hverju ferðu ekki þangað og athugar það?
Hrafnhildur:	Jú, ég ætla að gera það.
Gunnar:	Nennirðu að fara svo í búðina á leiðinni heim? Okkur vantar mjólk. Það er engin mjólk í ísskápnum.
Hrafnhildur:	Já, ekkert mál. Ég skal gera það. En ert þú með bíllykilinn minn?

Dialogue: Where is my cell phone?

Hrafnhildur:	Gunnar, where is my cell phone?
Gunnar:	Isn't it in the kitchen? I saw it on the kitchen table.
Hrafnhildur:	No, it's not there. I have looked everywhere. I have even looked in the fridge and under the sink.
Gunnar:	But have you looked in the living room or in the bedroom?
Hrafnhildur:	Yes, I have looked everywhere in the apartment.
Gunnar:	Did you forget it at work? You often forget your cell phone on your table. You are so forgetful!
Hrafnhildur:	Me? I'm not forgetful, not at all! It's you who forgets everything all the time. Do you remember when you lost your credit card downtown and we had to look and look for many hours?
Gunnar:	Yes, that was me, but that was just once. You lose something every day. I'm always helping you find your keys, your phone, your bag, your wallet, and even your glasses. When do you think you will lose your self?
Hrafnhildur:	Oh, stop making fun of me. You know I'm very sensitive.
Gunnar:	Yes, I am sorry. You know that I just enjoy making fun of you.
Hrafnhildur:	Maybe the phone is just at work, on my desk or in the common room. I was talking on the phone today before I left from there. I'm almost sure that it is there.
Gunnar:	Yes, why don't you go and check if it's there?
Hrafnhildur:	Yes, I'm going to do that.
Gunnar:	Could you stop by the store then on the way home? We need milk. There is no milk in the fridge.
Hrafnhildur:	Yes, no problem. I will do that. But do you have my car key?

Orðaforði – Vocabulary

af hverju why
alls enginn none at all
alls staðar *adv.* everywhere
annað hvort ... eða *conj.* either ... or
að athuga *v1* to check
á hverjum degi every day
á leiðinni on the way
áður *adv.* before
bíllykill *n. m.* car key
ekkert mál no problem
eldhúsborð *n. neu.* kitchen table
engin *pron. f.* no, not any
eiginlega *adv.* almost, actually
einu sinni once
farsími *n. m.* cellular phone
að gera grín to make fun
gleraugu *n. neu. pl.* glasses
að gleyma *v2* to forget
að grínast *v1 st-form* to poke fun
að hjálpa *v1* to help
íbúð *n. f.* apartment
ísskápur *n. m.* refrigerator
kaffistofa *n. f.* common room

klukkutími *n. m.* hour
kreditkort *n. neu.* credit card
að leita *v1* to search
lykill *n. m.* key
manstu *v. 2nd pers. past, see* **að muna**
meira að segja even
að muna *v. irr.* (**ég man**) to remember
oft *adv.* often
sé *v. irr. subj., see* **að vera**
sími *n. m.* telephone
sjálf *pron. f.* self
skal *v. irr., see* **skulu**
skulu *v. irr.* shall, will
stofa *n. f.* living room
svefnherbergi *n. neu.* bedroom
að týna *v2* to lose
undir *prep.* under
vaskur *n. m.* sink
veist *2nd pers., see* **að vita**
viðkvæm *adj. f.* sensitive
vinna *n. f.* work
að vita *v. irr.* (**ég veit**) to know

Orðasambönd – Useful expressions

Hvert ertu að fara?   Where are you going?

Ég er að fara ...   I'm going ...
    í bæinn.   downtown.
    í búð.   to the store.
    í skólann.   to school.
    til útlanda.   abroad.
    heim.   home.
    í sund.   to the pool.
    út að hlaupa.   out running.
    út að skemmta mér.   out to party.

Hvar ertu?	Where are you?
Ég er …	I'm …
í bænum.	downtown.
í búðinni.	in the store.
í skólanum.	in school.
í útlöndum.	abroad.
heima.	at home.
í sundi.	by the pool.
úti að hlaupa.	outside running.
úti að skemmta mér.	out partying.

Adverbs: Location and movement

Adverbs describing location have three forms. One refers to being in a place, the second a movement to the place, and the third one a movement from a place:

Location	Movement to a location	Movement from a location
heim home	**heim-a** at home	**að heim-an** from home
út out	**út-i** outside	**að ut-an** from outside/abroad

Hrafnhildur fer *að heiman* **klukkan átta.**	Hrafnhildur leaves *(from)* home at eight o'clock.
Gunnar er *heima.*	Gunnar is at home.
Hrafnhildur kemur *heim* **klukkan fimm.**	Hrafnhildur comes home at five o'clock.

The declension of the definite article in accusative and dative

The declension of the definite article is shown in italics in the chart below.

	Singular Definite Article		
	bíl/l (car)	**íbúð** (apartment)	**hús** (house)
	Masculine	**Feminine**	**Neuter**
nom. sing.	bíl-l-*inn*	íbúð-*in*	hús-*ið*
acc. sing.	bíl-*inn*	íbúð-*ina*	hús-*ið*
dat. sing.	bíl-*num*	íbúð-*inni*	hús-*inu*

Plural Definite Article

	bíl/ar (cars)	íbúð/ir (apartments)	hús (houses)
	Masculine	**Feminine**	**Neuter**
nom. pl.	bíl-ar-*nir*	íbúð-ir-*nar*	hús-*in*
acc. pl.	bíl-a-*na*	íbúð-ir-*nar*	hús-*in*
dat. pl.	bíl-u-*num*	íbúð-u-*num*	hús-u-*num*

Accusative:	**Ég er að fara í vinn-u-*na*.**	I'm going to work.
Dative:	**Farsíminn er í bíl-*num*.**	The cell is in the car.
	Tölvan mín er í eldhús-i-*nu*.	My computer is in the kitchen.

Although the usage of the definite article in Icelandic is similar to the usage in English, you will notice that it is not always the same. In the first example, **vinna** *work* has the definite form in Icelandic but not in English.

The declension of the definite article follows a similar pattern as that of the possessive pronouns (see Lesson 12).

Þetta er bíll*inn* m*inn*.	This is my car.
Ég er í bíl*num* m*ínum*.	I am in my car.

Dative referring to location with the prepositions *í* (in) and *á* (on)

One of the main functions of the dative is to express *location*. When you want to say that someone or something is located somewhere you use a preposition such as **í** *in* or **á** *on*, followed by the location in the dative case:

Ég bý á Ísland-*i*.	I live in Iceland.
Tanja býr í Rússland-*i*.	Tanya lives in Russia.

You also use dative when you want to say that someone is wearing something, since they are in the clothing:

Hann er í peys-*u* og bux-*um*.	He is wearing a sweater and pants.

The noun referring to the location can be in either the definite or the indefinite form, depending on the context.

Location versus movement: *í* (in) and *á* (on)

In this chapter, we have been looking at the use of the prepositions **í** and **á** followed by the dative case. The same prepositions may also take accusative. When they are followed by accusative, the phrases signify a movement *towards* a location rather than a state *in* a location.

Accusative: **í ísskáp-*inn***   **í vinn-*u-na***   **í eldhús-*ið***

Ég set smjörið í ísskápinn.	I put the butter in the fridge.
Ég ætla að fara í vinnuna.	I am going to go to work.
Ég fer í eldhúsið til að búa til kaffi.	I am going to the kitchen to make coffee.

Notice that all these examples involve motion: the butter is put *in* the fridge; I am going *to* work; I am going *to* the kitchen.

Dative: **í ísskáp-*num***   **í vinn-*u-nni***   **í eldhús-*inu***

Smjörið er í ísskápnum.	The butter is in the fridge.
Ég er í vinnunni.	I am at work.
Ég er í eldhúsinu að búa til kaffi.	I am in the kitchen making coffee.

Notice that all these examples involve the verb **vera** *to be* and that they refer to states. No motion is occurring: the butter *is* in the fridge; I *am* at work; I *am* in the kitchen.

Here are more examples of pairs and their meanings:

a)	**Ég set mjólk í ísskáp-inn.**	I put milk in the fridge.
b)	**Það er mjólk í ísskáp-num.**	There is milk in the fridge.

a)	**Ég fer í peys-u-na.**	I put the sweater on.
b)	**Ég er í peys-u-nni.**	I am wearing the sweater.

a)	**Við förum í eldhús-ið.**	We go to the kitchen.
b)	**Við borðum í eldhús-i-nu.**	We eat in the kitchen.

Æfingar – Exercises

1. **Fill in the blanks. Use the dative, definite form of the following words:**

   eldhúsið (the kitchen)
   borðstofan (the dining room)
   stofan (the living room)
   svefnherbergið (the bedroom)
   þvottahúsið (the laundry room)
   baðherbergið (the bathroom)
   skrifstofan (the study)
   forstofan (the entrance hall)
   sjónvarpsherbergið (the TV room)

   Stofuborðið er í _____
   Stofuborðið er í stofunni.

   a. Ísskápurinn er í   _____
   b. Rúmið er í   _____
   c. Vaskurinn er í   _____
   d. Sjónvarpið er í   _____
   e. Klósettið er á   _____
   f. Bakaraofninn er í   _____
   g. Baðkerið er á   _____
   h. Eldhússtóllinn er í   _____
   i. Sófinn er í   _____
   j. Tölvan er á   _____
   k. Sófaborðið er í   _____
   l. Þvottavélin er í   _____
   m. Sturtan er á   _____

2. Answer the questions using the words within parentheses:

Hvar er kisan ykkar? (í + eldhússkápur)
Kisan okkar er í eldhússkápnum.

a. Hvar eru eldspýturnar? (í + skúffa)

_____

b. Hvar er veskið mitt? (á + stofuborðið)

_____

c. Hvar eru lyklarnir mínir? (í + vasinn þinn)

_____

d. Hvar er kjötið? (á + grillið)

_____

e. Hvar er mamma? (í + bankinn)

_____

f. Hvar eru peningarnir mínir? (í + kommóðan)

_____

g. Hvar er maturinn? (á + borðstofuborðið)

_____

h. Hvar er fartölvan mín? (í + taskan)

_____

i. Hvar er kremið? (á + náttborðið)

_____

j. Hvar er súkkulaðið? (í + sjoppan)

_____

3. Fill in the blanks with the correct form of the verb *að gleyma*:

a. Við _____ að borga fyrir matinn.

b. Hrafnhildur og Gunnar _____ að hringja í Jeremy.

c. Hrafnhildur _____ oft símanum í vinnunni.

d. Ég _____ alltaf afmælinu þínu!

e. Þú _____ að kaupa í matinn.

f. Gunnar _____ oft að segja takk.

g. Vinir mínir _____ mér oft.

h. Þið _____ að læra heima.

i. Hver _____ alltaf að vaska upp?

j. Jeremy _____ fartölvunni sinni í skólanum.

4. Write sentences using the following words:

Maðurinn minn + gleyma + bíllinn + vinnan
Maðurinn minn gleymir bílnum í vinnunni.

a. Stelpan + gleyma + bókin + skólinn

_____

b. Ég + gleyma + þú

_____

c. Við + gleyma + tölva + borðið

_____

d. Hún + gleyma + penni + taskan

_____

e. Þið + gleyma + veski + strætó

_____

LESSON 14

Ég mun sakna þín!

◇◇◇◇◇◇

I will miss you!

Samtal: Ég mun sakna þín!

Hrafnhildur er að fara til Parísar í dag. Fyrst ætlar hún að fara á ráðstefnu þar sem hún mun halda erindi um íslenska myndlist. Þegar hún er búin að því ætlar hún að njóta lífsins í París. Hún ætlar að fara á söfn, sitja á kaffihúsum, fara út að borða og skoða myndlistarsýningar. Hún hlakkar mjög til ferðarinnar, því hún hefur aldrei áður komið til Frakklands. Hrafnhildur fer klukkan sjö í kvöld. Gunnar keyrir hana til Keflavíkur.

Gunnar:	Æi, Hrafnhildur mín, ekki fara. Ekki fara til Frakklands!
Hrafnhildur:	Ég kem aftur elskan mín. Ég verð bara í tvær vikur.
Gunnar:	En það er eins og heil eilífð. Ég mun sakna þín svo mikið.
Hrafnhildur:	Já, ég mun sakna þín líka, en reyndu bara að njóta lífsins á meðan. Farðu bara í heimsókn til mömmu þinnar eða til Halldórs vinar þíns.
Gunnar:	Ég vil ekki fara í heimsókn til þeirra, ég vil bara vera með þér.
Hrafnhildur:	Æi, Gunnar minn, þú veist að það er ekki hægt. Það er svo dýrt að fljúga á milli Íslands og Frakklands.
Gunnar:	Ætlarðu að senda mér póstkort frá Frakklandi?
Hrafnhildur:	Já, auðvitað sendi ég þér póstkort. Ég skal senda þér póstkort um leið og ég kem til Parísar.
Gunnar:	Og hvenær kemurðu svo aftur til landsins?
Hrafnhildur:	Ég kem aftur eftir nákvæmlega tvær vikur. Ég lendi klukkan sjö um kvöldið og ég verð komin til Reykjavíkur um níuleytið.
Gunnar:	Og ertu með allt sem þú ætlar að taka með þér?
Hrafnhildur:	Já, ég held það.
Gunnar:	Ertu með flugmiðann, vegabréfið og kortið?
Hrafnhildur:	Já, ég er með allt sem ég ætla að taka með mér.
Gunnar:	Allt nema þetta hérna. Hér er smá gjöf til þín.

Dialogue: I will miss you!

Hrafnhildur is going to Paris today. She is going to a conference to give a paper on Icelandic art. When she has finished doing that she is going to enjoy life in the city. She is going to visit museums, sit in cafés, go out to eat, and look at art exhibits. She looks forward to the trip because she has never been to France before. Hrafnhildur leaves at seven tonight. Gunnar is driving her to Keflavik.

Gunnar:	Oh, Hrafnhildur, don't go. Don't go to France!
Hrafnhildur:	I'll be back darling. I will just be away for two weeks.
Gunnar:	But that feels like an eternity. I'm going to miss you so much.
Hrafnhildur:	Yes, I will miss you too, but just try to enjoy life while I'm away. Just go and visit your mom or your friend Halldór.
Gunnar:	I don't want to visit them. I just want to be with you.
Hrafnhildur:	Oh, Gunnar, you know it's not possible. It's so expensive to fly from Iceland to France.
Gunnar:	Are you going to send me a postcard from France?
Hrafnhildur:	Yes, of course I will send you a postcard. I will send you a postcard immediately when I arrive in Paris.
Gunnar:	And when are you going to be back in the country?
Hrafnhildur:	I'll be back in exactly two weeks. I will land at seven o'clock in the evening, and I'll be in Reykjavik around nine.
Gunnar:	And do you have everything that you were going to bring?
Hrafnhildur:	Yes, I think so.
Gunnar:	Do you have the flight ticket, your passport, and your credit card?
Hrafnhildur:	Yes, I have everything that I was going to bring.
Gunnar:	Everything except this. Here is a small gift for you.

Gunnar réttir Hrafnhildi lítinn rauðan pakka.

Hrafnhildur:	Er þetta til mín? En sætt af þér!
Gunnar:	Nei, þetta er ekkert merkilegt. Bara eitthvað smáræði svo að þú gleymir mér ekki.

Hrafnhildur opnar pakkann. Í honum er falleg mynd af Gunnari og Hrafnhildi.

Hrafnhildur:	Ó, Gunnar, mikið er þetta sæt mynd! Þakka þér kærlega fyrir.
Gunnar:	Það var lítið. Lofarðu þá að koma aftur til mín?
Hrafnhildur:	Já, elskan mín, auðvitað kem ég aftur. Ég mun sakna þín mjög mikið.
Gunnar:	Bless, elskan mín!
Hrafnhildur	Bless bless! Sjáumst eftir tvær vikur!

Gunnar hands Hrafnhildur a small red package.

| Hrafnhildur: | Is this for me? How sweet of you! |
| Gunnar: | No, this is nothing special. Just something small so you don't forget me. |

Hrafnhildur opens up the package. Inside is a beautiful photo of Gunnar and Hrafnhildur.

| Hrafnhildur: | Oh, Gunnar, this is such a sweet photo! Thank you so much. |

Gunnar:	It was nothing. Do you promise to come back to me then?
Hrafnhildur:	Yes, darling, of course I will be back. I will miss you so much.
Gunnar:	Goodbye darling!
Hrafnhildur	Bye, bye! See you in two weeks!

Orðaforði – Vocabulary

auðvitað *adv.* of course
á meðan during that time
áður *adv.* before
dýrt *adj. neu.* expensive
eilífð *n. f.* eternity
eitthvað *pron. neu.* something
erindi *n. neu.* paper, talk
farðu! *v4 imp.* go!
ferð *n. f.* trip
flugmiði *n. m.* plane ticket
flugvél *n. f.* airplane
gjöf *n. f.* gift
að gleyma *v2* to forget
að halda *v3* **(ég held)** to think, to
    assume, to give (a paper)
að halda erindi to give a paper
heil *adj. f.* whole
heimsókn *n. f.* visit
held *v3, see* **að halda**
Keflavík *n. f.* Keflavik, the town where
    Iceland's international airport is
    located
að keyra *v2* to drive
kort *n. neu.* (credit) card

land *n. neu.* country (here: Iceland)
að lenda *v2* to land
lítill *adj. m.* small
lítinn *adj. m. acc., see* **lítill**
að lofa *v1* to promise
mun → **munu** *v. irr.* will
myndlistarsýning *n. f.* art exhibit
nákvæmlega *adv.* exactly
nema *conj.* except
níuleytið *n. neu.* around nine o'clock
að njóta *v3* **(ég nýt)** to enjoy
að opna *v1* to open
París *n. f.* Paris
póstkort *n. neu.* postcard
rauður *adj. m.* red
ráðstefna *n. f.* conference
safn *n. neu.* museum
að sakna *v1* to miss
skulu *v. irr.* shall
smáræði *n. neu.* something small
sætt *adj. neu.* sweet
að taka *v3* **(ég tek)** to take
vegabréf *n. neu.* passport
vika *n. f.* week

Orðasambönd – Useful expressions

The verb **gleyma** *to forget* takes the dative:

Ekki gleyma ...	Don't forget ...
vegabréfinu þínu.	your passport.
flugmiðanum.	the airline ticket.
tannburstanum.	the toothbrush.
tannkreminu.	the toothpaste.
peningaveskinu þínu.	your wallet.
kreditkortinu þínu.	your credit card.
góða skapinu!	your good mood!
mér!	me!

The verb **sakna** *to miss* takes the genitive:

Ég sakna ...	I miss ...
mömmu og pabba.	mom and dad.
allra vina minna.	all my friends.
Íslands.	Iceland.
þín.	you.
kærustunnar minnar.	my girlfriend.
kærastans míns.	my boyfriend.

Genitive

The fourth and final case in Icelandic is called the genitive. This is the case that you use when showing possession. In English, this is denoted with an apostrophe-*s*, as in *Donald's car*. In Icelandic, the genitive is also used in some other instances. We shall learn these in this chapter.

How to use the genitive

1. With certain verbs

There are a few verbs that take the genitive, for example **sakna** *miss* and **njóta** *enjoy*. This means that their objects are always in the genitive.

Ég nýt lífsins.	I enjoy life.
Ég sakna þín.	I miss you.

2. With certain prepositions

Some prepositions always take the genitive:

til to	**á milli** in between
milli between	**án** without

Examples:

Ég fer til Íslands.	I am going to Iceland.
Stofan er á milli eldhússins	The living room is between the
og svefnherbergisins.	kitchen and the bedroom.

3. To show possession

The genitive is used to show possession, just like English uses apostrophe-*s*. In Icelandic, the person or thing that is the owner or possessor is put into the genitive:

Höfuðborg Íslands heitir Reykjavík.	The capital of Iceland is called Reykjavik.
Þetta er bíll Halldórs.	This is Halldór's car.
Listasafn Reykjavíkur	Reykjavik Art Gallery

Usually both the genitive and the possessive pronoun are used to express possession when the possessor is a person:

Þetta er bíllinn *hans* Halldórs.	This is Halldór's car.
Mamma *hans* Jóns fer út í búð.	Jón's mother goes to the store.

Thus, in Icelandic you literally say *Mother his John's* for *John's mother*.

4. In Icelandic last names

As we have already learned, Icelanders use a patronymic or matronymic naming system. Thus, Icelanders do not have proper last names. An Icelander's patronym or matronym is formed by using a person's father's or mother's first name in the genitive followed by the word **son** or **dóttir** depending on whether the person is a man or a woman.

If **Gunnar** had a son named **Jón**, his son's name would be:

Jón Gunnarsson	Jón, son of Gunnar

Gunnar in the genitive is **Gunnars**. Then add the word *son* to form *Gunnarsson.*

5. In some compound words

The genitive is also used in some compound words. For example, the word **myndlistarsýning** means *art exhibit*. The possessive connotation comes from the fact that *art exhibit* can be rephrased as *an exhibit of art*. *Of art* has a genitive or possessive meaning, and in Icelandic the genitive form of **myndlist** is used within the compound **myndlist-*ar* sýning**.

Strong nouns in the genitive

The inflectional ending of the genitive is added to the stem. The endings in the singular are as follows:

Singular Case Endings of Strong Nouns

	Masculine hund/ur (dog) vin/ur (friend)		Feminine mynd (picture)	Neuter barn (child)
nom. sing.	hund-*ur*	vin-*ur*	mynd–	barn–
acc. sing.	hund–	vin–	mynd–	barn–
dat. sing.	hund-*i*	vin-*i*	mynd–	barn-*i*
gen. sing.	hund-*s*	vin-*ar*	mynd-*ar*	barn-*s*

The chart above shows a simplified version of the declension of nouns. There are many exceptions to these rules, such as the feminine noun **vík** *bay* which adds **ur** in genitive. Thus the genitive form of **Reykjavík** is **Reykjavíkur**. You can find the genitive singular in the glossary at the back of this book. Nouns are normally glossed as follows:

hund/ur (-s, -ar) *n. m.* dog

The first ending shown after the slash is the *nominative singular*; the first ending inside the brackets is the *genitive singular*; the second ending is the *nominative plural*.

Weak nouns in the genitive

The genitive of weak nouns is easy to memorize in singular since it is exactly the same as the accusative and dative:

Singular Case Endings of Weak Nouns

	Masculine pabb/i (dad)	Feminine klukk/a (clock)	Neuter aug/a (eye)
nom. sing.	pabb-*i*	klukk-*a*	aug-*a*
acc. sing.	pabb-*a*	klukk-*u*	aug-*a*
dat. sing.	pabb-*a*	klukk-*u*	aug-*a*
gen. sing.	pabb-*a*	klukk-*u*	aug-*a*

Ég sakna pabb-*a* og mömm-*u*. I miss mom and dad.

Plural nouns in the genitive

As mentioned, the inflectional ending of the genitive is added to the stem. The endings in the plural are as follows:

Plural Case Endings of Strong Nouns

	Masculine hund/ar (dogs) vin/ir (friends)		Feminine mynd/ir (pictures) klukk/ur (clocks)		Neuter börn (children) aug/u (eyes)	
nom. pl.	hund-*ar*	vin-*ir*	mynd-*ir*	klukk-*ur*	börn	aug-*u*
acc. pl.	hund-*a*	vin-*i*	mynd-*ir*	klukk-*ur*	börn	aug-*u*
dat. pl.	hund-*um*	vin-*um*	mynd-*um*	klukk-*um*	börn-*um*	aug-*um*
gen. pl.	hund-*a*	vin-*a*	mynd-*a*	klukk-*na*	barn-*a*	aug-*na*

Definite article in the genitive

The genitive of the definite article is as follows. Note that the second **n** is dropped in the masculine singular definite article in the genitive, while the feminine singular definite article gains an **n**.

Singular Definite Article with Singular Strong Nouns

	Masculine hund/ur (dog)	Feminine mynd (picture)	Neuter barn (child)
nom. sing.	hund-*ur-inn*	mynd-*in*	barn-*ið*
acc. sing.	hund-*inn*	mynd-*ina*	barn-*ið*
dat. sing.	hund-*i-num*	mynd-*inni*	barn-*i-nu*
gen. sing.	hund-*s-ins*	mynd-*ar-innar*	barn-*s-ins*

Plural Definite Article with Plural Strong Nouns

	Masculine hund/ar (dogs)	Feminine mynd/ir (pictures)	Neuter börn (children)
nom. pl.	hund-*ar-nir*	mynd-*ir-nar*	börn-*in*
acc. pl.	hund-*a-na*	mynd-*ir-nar*	börn-*in*
dat. pl.	hund-*u-num*	mynd-*u-num*	börn-*u-num*
gen. pl.	hund-*a-nna*	mynd-*a-nna*	barn-*a-nna*

Examples:

Ég nýt líf-*s*-*ins*.   I enjoy life.
Hrafnhildur nýtur   Hrafnhildur enjoys the
    sumarfrí-*s*-*ins*.   summer holiday.

Personal pronouns in the genitive

The genitive of the personal pronouns is as follows:

Nominative & Genitive of the Personal Pronouns

Person	Singular			Plural	
	Nom.		**Gen.**	**Nom.**	**Gen.**
1st	ég	I	mín my	við we	okkar our
2nd	þú	you	þín your	þið you	ykkar your
3rd *m.*	hann	he	hans his	þeir they	
f.	hún	she	hennar her	þær they	þeirra their
neu.	það	it	þess its	þau they	

Examples:

Þetta er bara á milli *mín* og *þín*.   This is just between me and you.
Þessi pakki er til *hennar*.   This package is for her.

Possessives in the genitive

The possessive pronouns decline in the following way:

Singular:

Genitive of the Possessive Pronouns
minn/þinn/sinn (my/mine/your, yours/his, hers, its)

	Masculine	Feminine	Neuter
nom. sing.	minn/þinn/sinn	mín/þín/sín	mitt/þitt/sitt
acc. sing.	minn/þinn/sinn	mín-a/þín-a/sín-a	mitt/þitt/sitt
dat. sing.	mín-um/þín-um/ sín-um	minn-i/þinn-i/sinn-i	mín-u/þín-u/sín-u
gen. sing.	míns/þíns/síns	minnar/þinnar/sinnar	míns/þíns/síns

Plural:

Genitive of the Possessive Pronouns

mínir/þínir/sínir (our, ours/your, yours/their, theirs)

	Masculine	Feminine	Neuter
nom. pl.	mín-ir/þín-ir/sín-ir	mín-ar/þín-ar/sín-ar	mín/þín/sín
acc. pl.	mín-a/þín-a/sín-a	mín-ar/þín-ar/sín-ar	mín/þín/sín
dat. pl.	mín-um/þín-um/sín-um		
gen. pl.	minna/þinna/sinna		

Þetta er til mömmu *minnar.*	This is for my mom.
Ég sakna hund*sins míns.*	I miss my dog.
Hann saknar barn*anna sinna.*	He misses his children.

Modal verbs: *munu* (will) and *skulu* (shall)

The modals **munu** *will* and **skulu** *shall* are both used to express future tense.

munu (will)

Person	Singular			Plural		
1st	ég	**mun**	I will	við	**mun-*um***	we will
2nd	þú	**mun-*t***	you will	þið	**mun-*uð***	you will
3rd *m.*	hann		he	þeir		
f.	hún	**mun**	she will	þær	**mun-*u***	they will
neu.	það		it	þau		

skulu (shall)

Person	Singular			Plural		
1st	ég	**skal**	I shall	við	**skul-*um***	we shall
2nd	þú	**skal-*t***	you shall	þið	**skul-*uð***	you shall
3rd *m.*	hann		he	þeir		
f.	hún	**skal**	she shall	þær	**skul-*u***	they shall
neu.	það		it	þau		

Munu (will)

The modal **munu** is a more formal way of showing future tense than the verb **ætla** which you have learned before. While the verb **ætla** shows strong intentions, the verb **munu** implies that something is inevitable. It is also used when you are giving a *solemn promise*, that is when you are promising someone that you will never forget them, but not when you promise to do the dishes.

Ég mun aldrei gleyma þér.	I will never forget you.
Hann mun aldrei fyrirgefa mér.	He will never forgive me.

Note that **munu** is a modal verb so that the verb following it has no infinitive marker **að**. You say **ég mun aldrei að gleyma þér** *I will never forget you.*

Skulu (shall)

Skulu is used in the following contexts:

As a promise:

Ég skal koma aftur.	I will come back *(I promise).*
Ég skal vaska upp.	I will do the dishes.
Ég skal aldrei gleyma þér.	I will never forget you *(that's a promise).*

Or as a threat:

Ég skal ná þér!	I'll get you!
Þú skalt sjá eftir þessu!	You will regret this!

Or as a plural imperative with a promissory tone:

Við skulum fara.	Let's go *(we will go, don't worry).*

Að hlakka til (to look forward to)

The phrase **að hlakka til** *to look forward to* is either followed by a noun in genitive or an infinitive phrase:

Hrafnhildur hlakkar til *ferðarinnar.*	Hrafnhildur looks forward to the trip.
Gunnar hlakkar til *frísins.*	Gunnar looks forward to the vacation.
Ég hlakka til *að fara* **til Parísar!**	I look forward to going to Paris!

Æfingar – Exercises

1. Make pairs of personal pronouns:

Nominative	Genitive
þú	hennar
við	ykkar
hann	þeirra
þær	mín
hún	hans
það	þín
ég	okkar
þið	þess

2. Put the nouns into the genitive:

a) Lampinn er á milli _____ og _____ (borð, stóll)

b) Stóllinn er á milli _____ og _____ (sjónvarp, sófi)

c) Sófinn er á milli _____ og _____ (lampi, gluggi)

d) Ég sit á milli _____ og _____ (Óli, Heiða)

3. Put the following nouns and possessives into the genitive:

Ég sakna:

a. pabbi minn _____

b. mamma mín _____

c. strákurinn _____

d. stelpan _____

e. húsið mitt _____

f. íbúðin mín _____

g. landið mitt _____

h. tölvan mín _____

4. Translate the following sentences using *munu* and *skulu*:

a. I will never go (that's a promise)!

_____

b. Let me help you.

_____

c. I shall learn Icelandic!

_____

d. I will cook tonight.

_____

e. He will never forget her.

_____

GRAMMAR SUMMARY

Declension of nouns

Masculine Nouns

The following endings are added to the stem of masculine nouns.

		Strong		Weak	
		Inflectional ending	Definite article	Inflectional ending	Definite article
Singular	nom.	ur/l/n/r	inn	i	nn
	acc.	–	inn	a	nn
	dat.	(i)	num	a	num
	gen.	s[1]	ins	a	ns
Plural	nom	ar[2]	nir	ar	nir
	acc.	a[3]	na	a	na
	dat.	u(m) (a→ö)	num	u(m) (a→ö)	num
	gen.	a	nna	a	nna

1. Some masculine nouns end in *ar* in genitive singular, e.g. *vinur→vinar* 'friend's.'
2. Some masculine nouns end in *ir* in nominative plural, e.g. *vinur→vinir* 'friends' and *gestur→gestir* 'guests.'
3. The nouns that have an *ir* ending in nominative plural have an *i* ending in accusative plural, e.g. *vinir→vini* 'friends.'

Feminine Nouns

The following endings are added to the stem of feminine nouns:

		Strong		Weak	
		Inflectional ending	Definite article	Inflectional ending	Definite article
Singular	nom.	–	in	a	n
	acc.	–	ina	u (a→ö)	na
	dat.	–	inni	u (a→ö)	nni
	gen.	ar	innar	u (a→ö)	nnar
Plural	nom	ir (ö→a)	nar	ur (a→ö)	nar
	acc.	ir (ö→a)	nar	ur (a→ö)	nar
	dat.	u(m)	num	u(m) (a→ö)	num
	gen.	(n)a (ö→a)	nna	(n)a	nna

193

Neuter Nouns

The following endings are added to the stem of neuter nouns.

		Strong		Weak	
		Inflectional ending	Definite article	Inflectional ending	Definite article
Singular	nom.	–	ið	a	ð
	acc.	–	ið	a	ð
	dat.	i	nu	a	nu
	gen.	s	ins	a	ns
Plural	nom	– (a→ö)	in	u (a→ö)	n
	acc.	– (a→ö)	in	u (a→ö)	n
	dat.	u(m) (a→ö)	num	u(m) (a→ö)	num
	gen.	a	nna	(n)a	nna

Declension of the irregular noun *maður* (man)

		Indefinite	Definite
Singular	nom.	mað-**ur**	mað-**ur-inn**
	acc.	mann	mann-**inn**
	dat.	mann-**i**	mann-**i-num**
	gen.	mann-**s**	mann-**s-ins**
Plural	nom.	menn	menn-**ir-nir**
	acc.	menn	menn-**ina**
	dat.	mönn-**um**	mönn-**u-num**
	gen.	mann-**a**	mann-**a-nna**

Declension of adjectives

The following endings are added to the stem of adjectives.

		Masculine	Feminine	Neuter
Singular	nom.	ur/l/n/r/–	– (a→ö)	t
	acc.	an	a	t
	dat.	um (a→ö)	ri[4] (lli, nni)[5]	u (a→ö)
	gen.	s	rar[4] (llar, nnar)[5]	s

Plural	**nom**	ir	ar	– (a→ö)
	acc.	a	ar	– (a→ö)
	dat.	um (a→ö)	um (a→ö)	um (a→ö)
	gen.	ra[1] (lla, nna)[2]	ra[1] (lla, nna)[2]	ra[4] (lla, nna)[5]

1. When an adjective stem ends in a vowel, such as *blá-r* 'blue,' the *r* is doubled: *blárra, blárri,* etc.
2. When adjectives end in *n* or *l*, such as in *gamal-l* 'old' or *feimin-n* 'shy,' the stem-ending and the inflectional endings assimilate and become *ll* and *nn*: *gamalla, feiminna.*

Personal and reflexive pronouns

		1ˢᵗ pers. I	**2ⁿᵈ pers.** you	**3ʳᵈ pers.** (*m.*) he	**3ʳᵈ pers.** (*f.*) she	**3ʳᵈ pers.** (*neu.*) it	**Reflexive** oneself
Singular	**nom.**	ég	þú	hann	hún	það	
	acc.	mig	þig	hann	hana	það	sig
	dat.	mér	þér	honum	henni	því	sér
	gen.	mín	þín	hans	hennar	þess	sín

Plural	**nom.**	við	þið	þeir	þær	þau	
	acc.	okkur	ykkur	þá	þær	þau	sig
	dat.	okkur	ykkur	þeim	þeim	þeim	sér
	gen.	okkar	ykkar	þeirra	þeirra	þeirra	sín

Possessive pronouns

		1ˢᵗ person			**2ⁿᵈ person**		
		m.	**f.**	**neu.**	**m.**	**f.**	**neu.**
Singular	**nom.**	minn	mín	mitt	þinn	þín	þitt
	acc.	minn	mína	mitt	þinn	þína	þitt
	dat.	mínum	minni	mínu	þínum	þinni	þínu
	gen.	míns	minnar	míns	þíns	þinnar	þíns

		1st person			2nd person		
		m.	f.	neu.	m.	f.	neu.
Plural	nom.	mínir	mínar	mín	þínir	þínar	þín
	acc.	mína	mínar	mín	þína	þínar	þín
	dat.	mínum	mínum	mínum	þínum	þínum	þínum
	gen.	minna	minna	minna	þinna	þinna	þinna

Declension of numbers

einn (one)

		m.	f.	neu.
Singular	nom.	einn	ein	eitt
	acc.	einn	eina	eitt
	dat.	einum	einni	einu
	gen.	eins	einnar	eins

tveir (two)

		m.	f.	neu.
Plural	nom.	tveir	tvær	tvö
	acc.	tvo	tvær	tvö
	dat.	tveimur	tveimur	tveimur
	gen.	tveggja	tveggja	tveggja

þrír (three)

		m.	f.	neu.
Plural	nom.	þrír	þrjár	þrjú
	acc.	þrjá	þrjár	þrjú
	dat.	þremur	þremur	þremur
	gen.	þriggja	þriggja	þriggja

fjórir (four)

		m.	f.	neu.
Plural	nom.	fjórir	fjórar	fjögur
	acc.	fjóra	fjórar	fjögur
	dat.	fjórum	fjórum	fjórum
	gen.	fjögurra	fjögurra	fjögurra

EXERCISE KEY

Lesson 1

1. a) Hæ!, Blessaður!, Sæll!, Blessaður og sæll!. b) Góðan dag! Góðan daginn! c) Gott kvöld!, Góða kvöldið. d) Hæ! Blessuð! e) Hæ! Blessaðar! f) Sæl og blessuð! g) Góða nótt!
2. a) Ég heiti Hrafnhildur. b) Hún heitir Anna. c) Hann heitir Óli. d) Þau heita Anna og Óli. e) Við heitum Hrafnhildur og Óli. f) Þær heita Anna og Hrafnhildur.
3. a) þeir, b) hún, c) hann, d) við, e) þið, f) þau.
4. A: Góðan daginn!
   B: Góðan dag!
   A: Hvað heitir þú?
   B: Ég heiti Anna Jónsdóttir.
   A: Heitir Þú Anna Ómarsdóttir?/Heitirðu Anna Ómarsdóttir?
   B: Nei, Anna Jónsdóttir.
   A: Fyrirgefðu.
   B: Ekkert mál.

Lesson 2

1. a) er, b) er, c) erum, d) ert, e) ert, f) er, g) erum, h) eruð.
2. a) tala, b) talar, c) tala, d) tala, e) tölum.
3. a) Þetta er Jón. Hann er að læra frönsku. b) Hrafnhildur er að tala íslensku. c) Þið eruð að læra íslensku. d) Talarðu frönsku? Talar þú frönsku?

Lesson 3

1. a) masc, b) fem, c) fem, d) masc, e) neu, f) masc, g) neu, h) masc, i) fem, j) masc, k) neu, l) neu, m) masc, n) masc, o) fem, p) masc, q) masc.
2. a) rómantísk, b) rómantískur, c) rómantísk, d) rómantískur, e) skemmtilegur, f) skemmtilegur, g) skemmtilegt, h) bandarískur, i) bandarísk, j) bandarískur.
3. a) Hann heitir ekki Óli. b) Þetta er íslenskur matur. c) Ísland er fallegt land. d) Þetta er ekki bakarí.
4. a) Ert þetta þú? b) Er þetta íslenskt skyr? c) Heitirðu Einar? Heitir þú Einar? d) Er hangikjöt reykt lambakjöt?

Lesson 4

1. a) íslensk, b) kanadísk, c) bandarískur, d) finnskur, e) frönsk, f) sænsk, g) þýskur, h) hollensk, i) austurrísk, j) pólskur, k) úkraínsk.
2. Þetta er Erna. Hún er íslensk. Hún er fædd og uppalin í Reykjavík. Og þetta er Ómar. Hann er leikari. Hann er ekki feiminn. Hann er alltaf kátur/glaður/hress/hamingjusamur. Þetta er Baldur. Hann er sagnfræðingur. Hann er mjög feiminn.
3. a) gult glas, b) brúnt hús, c) svart te, d) grænt te, e) grátt sjónvarp, f) dökkblá bók.
4. a) Pabbi (minn) er búinn að elda pasta. b) Hann er búinn að lesa. c) Jeremy er búinn að læra heima. d) Hrafnhildur er búin að fara í sturtu.
5. a) 2, b) 4, c) 7, d) 5, e) 1, f) 3, g) 6.

Lesson 5

1. a) sófinn, b) tölvan, c) lykillinn, d) íbúðin, e) gatan, f) eldhúsið, g) hundurinn, h) rúmið.
2. a) borg, b) kisa, c) hús, d) skyr, e) penni.
3. a) þinn, b) hennar, c) okkar, d) mín.
4. a) fjórir, b) sautján, c) tólf, d) tíu, e) fimm, f) fimm, g) þrír, h) núll.
5. a) Fimm sex einn, tveir þrír fjórir fimm. b) Fjórir þrír einn, fimm sex sjö fimm. c) Fjórir níu einn, fjórir einn fjórir fimm.
6. a) tvær, b) ein, c) þrír, d) fimm.

Lesson 6

1. a) borðar, b) borðum, c) borða, d) læri, e) lærir, f) læra, g) læra, h) vinn, i) vinnur, j) vinna, k) ferð, l) förum, m) fer, n) farið, o) búa, p) bý, q) búið, r) skilur, s) skiljum, t) skilja, u) skilja, v) skilur, w) skilur, x) skil, y) skilur, z) skilja.
2. a) Hún er þrjú. b) Hún er hálf eitt. c) Hún er korter í átta. d) Hún er korter yfir ellefu. e) Hún er þrjár mínútur í þrjú. Hana vantar þrjár mínútur í þrjú.
3. a) þriðjudagur, b) miðvikudögum, föstudögum, c) sunnudaginn, d) laugardaginn, e) þriðjudögum, fimmtudögum, f) miðvikudagur, g) þriðjudaginn.
4. a) Hvar er Gunnar? Hann er heima. b) Ég fer heim klukkan hálf sex. c) Mamma er ekki heima á laugardögum. d) Ég sef til ellefu á sunnudögum. e) Ég fer út klukkan hálf tíu. f) Við ætlum í leikhús á miðvikudagskvöld. Við förum í leikhús á miðvikudagskvöld.

Lesson 7

1. a) pabbar, b) töskur, c) tölvur, d) borð, e) hnífar, f) kort, g) lög, h) söngvarar, i) bílar, j) Kanadamenn, k) kettir.
2. a) glas, b) penni, c) barn, d) kennari, e) kisa, f) land, g) peningur, h) króna, i) dollari.
3. a) mörg, b) margar, c) margir, d) margir.
4. a) Hvað eru mörg hús hér? b) Hvað eru mörg börn hér? c) Hvað eru margir hestar hér? d) Hvað eru margir hér? Hvað er margt fólk hér?

Lesson 8

1. a) stelpur, stelpurnar, b) diskar, diskarnir, c) myndir, myndirnar, d) bækur, bækurnar, e) menn, mennirnir, f) konur, konurnar, g) börn, börnin, h) klukkur, klukkurnar, i) kettir, kettirnir, j) pennar, pennarnir, k) steinar, steinarnir, l) borgir, borgirnar.
2. a) Þetta eru tölvurnar mínar. b) Þetta eru svartir hundar. c) Hér eru grænir stólar. d) Hér eru skemmtilegir menn. e) Hér eru íslenskar konur. f) Hér eru sæt börn.
3. a) I'm going to the movies. b) You are going to leave. c) We are going to sleep. d) We go to sleep. e) We have been studying.

Lesson 9

1. a) kött, b) hníf, c) Ameríkana, d) kennara, e) vind, f) tölvu, g) möppu, h) bók, i) glas, j) sjónvarp, k) þjón, l) mat, m) veitingastað, n) bát.
2. a) tómat, banana, ost. b) kjúkling. c) pabba, afa, frænda. d) bíl. e) Íslending, Kanadamann.
3. a) Jeremy er mjög svangur núna. Hann fer á veitingastað. Hann pantar pítsu og súpu. b) Steingrímur ætlar að kaupa bíl. c) Jeremy er að læra íslensku. Hann talar líka ensku og þýsku. d) Sigga elskar Sigga.
4. a) Farðu!, farið!, (farið þið!, fariði!), b) borðaðu!, c) borgaðu!, borgið!, (borgið þið!, borgiði!), d) eldaðu!, eldið!, (eldið þið!, eldiði!), e) talaðu!, talið!, (talið þið!, taliði!), f) segðu!, segið!, (segið þið!, segiði!), g) kenndu!, kennið!, (kennið þið!, kenniði!).

Lesson 10

1. a) Pabbi kaupir tómat og ost. b) Við bökum köku. c) Bökum köku! d) Guðlaugur elskar Önnu. e) Anna elskar Árna. f) Ég sé Helgu, Hönnu, Nonna og Magga. g) Afi bakar pítsu. h) Grillum í kvöld! i) Ég er grænmetisæta. Ég borða bara grænmeti. j) Hvað eigum við að elda í kvöld?

2.   a) á, b) hefur, c) á, d) á, e) á, f) á.

3.   a) rauðan, fínan, b) bláa, hvíta, c) grænt, svart, d) leiðinlega.

4.   a) Nítján hundruð sjötíu og tvö. b) Nítján hundruð áttatíu og sjö. c) Tvö
     þúsund og tólf. d) Nítján hundruð fjörutíu og níu. e) Eitt þúsund tvö
     hundruð sextíu og sjö krónur f) hundrað og fimmtíu krónur, g) fimm
     hundruð og fimmtíu krónur, h) tvö þúsund þrjú hundruð sjötíu og ein
     króna, i) tuttugu dollarar, j) tólf dollarar, k) fjórir dollarar, l) hundrað
     fjörtíu og tveir dollarar.

Lesson 11

1.   a) bók, b) kisu, c) ömmu, d) bát or báti, e) hval, f) herbergi, g) stofu,
     h) tölvu, i) klukku, j) mat, k) glasi, l) rauðvíni, m) smjöri.

2.   a) mér, b) ykkur, c) þeim, d) henni, e) honum, f) mér.

3.   Þetta er Árný. Hún býr á Íslandi núna en hún bjó í þrjú ár á Englandi.
     Hún talar mjög góða ensku. Árný vinnur í skóla. Árný er mjög jákvæð
     og hress manneskja. Hún hefur mikinn áhuga á íþróttum, sérstaklega
     fótbolta og golfi.

Lesson 12

1.   a) Bróðir minn lánar mömmu bíl. b) Ég rétti þér salt og pipar. c) Amma
     sendir mér pakka. d) Kærastinn minn gefur mér kettling. e) Hrafnhildur
     kaupir gjöf handa Gunnari. f) Kennarinn segir mér sögu. g) Jeremy
     sendir okkur póstkort. h) Mamma kaupir penna, blýant og skólatösku
     handa mér. i) Ég gef pabba og mömmu hund.

2.   a) sjötti nóvember, b) fjórða mars, c) tuttugasta og þriðja ágúst,
     d) tuttugasta og fyrsta maí, e) þrítugasta maí, f) tuttugasti og fjórði
     desember.

Lesson 13

1.   a) eldhúsinu, b) svefnherberginu, c) eldhúsinu, (á) baðherberginu, (á)
     klósettinu, d) sjónvarpsherberginu, stofunni, e) baðherberginu,
     f) eldhúsinu, g) baðherberginu, h) eldhúsinu, i) stofunni,
     j) skrifstofunni, k) stofunni, l) þvottahúsinu, m) baðherberginu.

2.   a) Eldspýturnar eru í skúffunni. b) Veskið þitt er á stofuborðinu.
     c) Lyklarnir eru í vasanum þínum. d) Kjötið er á grillinu. e) Mamma
     er í bankanum. f) Peningarnir eru í kommóðunni. g) Maturinn er
     á borðstofuborðinu. h) Fartölvan þín er í töskunni. i) Kremið er á
     náttborðinu. j) Súkkulaðið er í sjoppunni.

3. a) gleymum, b) gleyma, c) gleymir, d) gleymi, e) gleymir, f) gleymir,
   g) gleyma, h) gleymið, i) gleymir, j) gleymir.
4. a) Stelpan gleymir bókinni í skólanum. b) Ég gleymi þér. c) Við
   gleymum tölvunni á borðinu. d) Hún gleymir pennanum í töskunni.
   e) Þið gleymið veskinu í strætó.

Lesson 14

1. þú – þín, við – okkar, hann – hans, þær – þeirra, hún – hennar,
   það – þess, ég – mín, þið – ykkar.
2. a) borðsins, stólsins, b) sjónvarpsins, sófans, c) lampans, gluggans,
   d) Óla, Heiðu.
3. a) pabba míns, b) mömmu minnar, c) stráksins, d) stelpunnar, e) hússins
   míns, f) íbúðarinnar minnar, g) landsins míns, h) tölvunnar minnar.
4. a) Ég mun aldrei fara! b) Ég skal hjálpa þér. c) Ég skal læra íslensku.
   d) Ég skal elda í kvöld. e) Hann mun aldrei gleyma henni.

Icelandic-English Glossary

Nouns are listed in their nominative singular form, with a slash separating the stem of the noun from its ending (if any). The gender of the noun is given, whether masculine *n. m*, feminine *n. f.*, or neuter *n. neu.* The genitive singular and nominative plural forms are given in parentheses after the Icelandic words. An asterisk (*) signifies that a particular form does not exist, and a dash (–) means that the plural form of a noun is identical with its nominative singular form.

For **adjectives** and **pronouns**, only the masculine forms are listed, but feminine and neuter forms are shown in paretheses if they undergo a vowel shift or other phonological changes.

Verbs are given in the infinitive and the conjugational pattern is given with numbers from 1–5. Imperatives and *st*-forms are listed separately.

aðeins *adv.* a bit
af *prep.* of
af hverju *inter.* why
af/i (-a, -ar) *n. m.* grandfather
afmæli (-s, –) *n. neu.* birthday
afmælisgjöf (-gjafar, gjafir) *n. f.* birthday present
afmælisveisl/a (-u, -ur) *n. f.* birthday party
að afsaka *v1* to excuse
aftur *adv.* again
all/ur (öll *f.*) *pron.* all, whole, entire
alls staðar *adv.* everywhere
alltaf *adv.* always
alveg *adv.* completely
alvörugefin/n *adj.* serious
Ameríkan/i (-a, -ar) *n. m.* American (referring to people)
amm/a (ömmu, ömmur) *n. f.* grandmother
ananas (-s, *) *n. m.* pineapple
annað hvort ... eða *conj.* either ... or

annar (önnur *f.* annað *neu.*) *pron.* another, second
appelsín/a (-u, -ur) *n. f.* orange
appelsínugul/ur *adj.* orange (color)
appelsínusaf/i (-a, -ar) *n. m.* orange juice
að athuga *v1* to check
auðvitað *adv.* of course
aug/a (-a, -u) *n. neu.* eye
auglýsing (-ar, -ar) *n. f.* advertisement
augnablik (-s, —) *n. neu.* one moment
austur (-s, *) *n. neu.* east
Austurland (-s,*) *n. neu.* east part of Iceland

á *prep.* on
á hverjum degi every day
ábót (-ar, -ir, -ar,*) *n. f.* seconds, a second helping
ábyggilega *adv.* surely
ábyrg/ur *adj.* responsible
áður *adv.* before

ágæt/ur *adj.* nice, fine
áhug/i (-a, *) *n. m.* interest
áhugamál (-s, –) *n. neu.* interest
að ákveða *v3* to decide
álegg (-s, –) *n. neu.* things to put on
    bread
ánægð/ur *adj.* pleased
ást (-ar, -ir) *n. f.* love

baðherbergi (-s, –) *n. neu.* bathroom
baðker (-s, –) *n. neu.* bath tub
að baka *v1* to bake
bakaraofn (-s, -ar) *n. m.* oven
bakpok/i (-a, -ar) *n. m.* back pack
banan/i (-a, -ar) *n. m.* banana
Bandaríkin *n. neu. (only in pl. def.)*
    USA
bandarísk/ur *adj.* from the USA
bara *adv.* just
barn (-s, börn) *n. neu.* child
báðir (báðar *f.* bæði *neu.*) *pron.* both
bát/ur (-s, -ar) *n. m.* boat
belti (-s, –) *n. neu.* belt
að bera *v4* to carry
best/ur *adj. super.* best
bindi (-s, –) *n. neu.* neck tie
bíddu! *v. imp.* wait!
bíl/l (-s, -ar) *n. m.* car
bíllykil/l (-s, -lyklar) *n. m.* car key
bíó (-s, –) *n. neu.* movie theater
bjart/ur (björt *f.*) *adj.* bright
að bjóða (ég býð) *v3* invite
bjór (-s, -ar) *n. m.* beer
blaðamað/ur (-manns, -menn) *n. m.*
    journalist
blank/ur (blönk *f.*) *adj.* broke
blá/r (blátt *neu.*) *adj.* blue
bleik/ur *adj.* pink
bless *interj.* good bye!
blessað/ur (blessuð *f.*) *adj.* hi! (*lit.*
    blessed)
blóm (-s, –) *n. neu.* flower
borð (-s, –) *n. neu.* table
að borða *v1* to eat
borðstof/a (-u, -ur) *n. f.* dining room
borg (-ar, -ir) *n. f.* city

að borga *v1* to pay
bók (-ar, bækur) *n. f.* book
bókmenntir *n. f. (only in pl.)* literature
brauð (-s, –) *n. neu.* bread
bráðum *adv.* soon
bróðir (bróður, bræður) *n. m.* brother
brún/n *adj.* brown
að búa (ég bý) *v5* live
búð (-ar, ir) *n. f.* shop
búðarborð (-s, –) *n. neu.* counter
búin/n (búið *neu.*) *adj.* finished
að byrja *v1* to start
bæ! *interj.* bye! (informal)
bæ/r (-jar, -ir) *n. m.* town, city center
bæði *pron. neu. pl.* both

dag/ur (-s, -ar) *n. m.* day
dansk/a (dönsku, *) *n. f.* Danish,
    referring to the language
dálítið *adv.* a bit
disk/ur (-s, -ar) *n. m.* plate, disc
djass (–, *) *n. m.* jazz
dollar/i (-a, -ar) *n. m.* dollar
dós (-ar, -ir) *n. f.* tin, can
dót (-s, –) *n. neu.* stuff, things
dóttir (dóttur, dætur) *n. f.* daughter
að drekka *v3* to drink
að dreyma *v2* (impersonal, to dream
    mig dreymir)
að drífa sig *v3* to hurry up, to get going
drop/i (-a, -ar) *n. m.* drop
dugleg/ur *adj.* diligent
dýn/a (-u, -ur) *n. f.* mattress
dýr *adj.* expensive
dökkhærð/ur *adj.* dark haired

ef *conj.* if
eftir *prep.* after, by
eftirrétt/ur (-ar, -ir) *n. m.* dessert
að eiga *v irr.* to have, to be supposed to
    do something
eiginlega *adv.* almost, actually, rather
eilífð (-ar, -ir) *n. f.* eternity
einhver *pron.* someone
einmitt *adv.* exactly
ein/n *num.* one

ein/n *adj.* alone
einsamal/l (-sömul *f.***)** *adj.* alone
einstakling/ur (-s, -ar) *n. m.* individual
einu sinni once
eitthvað *pron. neu.* something
ekkert *pron. neu.* nothing
ekkert mál no problem
ekki *adv.* not
að elda *v1* to cook
eldhús (-s, –) *n. neu.* kitchen
eldhúsborð (-s, –) *n. neu.* kitchen table
eldhússtól/l (-s, -ar) *n. m.* kitchen chair
eldspýt/a (-u, -ur) *n. f.* match
að elska *v1* to love
elska (-u, -ur) *n. f.* darling
en *conj.* but
engin/n (ekkert *neu.***)** *pron.* no one, nobody
enn *adv.* still
ensk/a (-u, *) *n. f.* English, referring to the language
epli (-s, –) *n. neu.* apple
erfið/ur (erfitt *neu.***)** *adj.* difficult
erindi (-s, –) *n. neu.* paper, talk
eyr/a (-a, -u) *n. neu.* ear

ég *pron.* I

falleg/ur *adj.* beautiful
að fara (ég fer) *v4* to go
að fara á fætur to get out of bed
að fara á hestbak to go horseback riding
að fara í sturtu to take a shower
farsím/i (-a, -ar) *n. m.* cell phone
fartölv/a (-u, -ur) *n. f.* laptop
fatabúð (-ar, -ir) *n. f.* fashion store
að fá (ég fæ) *v5* to get
feimin/n (feimið *neu.***)** *adj.* shy
ferð (-ar, -ir) *n. f.* trip
ferðalag (-s, ferðalög) *n. neu.* tour, trip
ferðamað/ur (-manns, -menn) *m. n.* tourist
að finnast *v. st-form (impersonal)* to think, to seem, to find
fimmtudagur (-s, -ar) *n. m.* Thursday

fisk/ur (-s, -ar) *n. m.* fish
fín/n *adj.* neat, nice
fjólublá/r (fjólublátt *neu.***)** *adj.* purple
fjörð/ur (fjarðar, firðir) *n. m.* fjord
fleira *adj. comp.* more
flott/ur *adj.* cool, great
flott! *adj.* cool! great!
flugmið/i (-a, -ar) *n. m.* plane ticket
flugvél (-ar, -ar) *n. f.* airplane
foreldr/ar *n. m. pl.* parents
forstof/a (-u, -ur) *n. f.* entrance hall
fólk *n. neu. (only in sing.)* people
fór *v. past, see* **að fara**
fótbolt/i (-a, -ar) *n. m.* soccer, soccer ball
franska (frönsku, *) *n. f.* French, referring to the language
frá *prep.* from
frábær *adj.* great
frátekin/n (frátekið *neu.***)** *adj.* reserved
franskar kartöflur *n. f. pl.* french fries
frekar *adv.* rather
að frétta *v2* to hear (news)
frið/ur (-ar, *) *n. m.* peace
frí (-s, frí) *n. neu.* vacation
að frumsýna *v2* to premier
frumsýning (-ar, -ar) *n. f.* premier
frænd/i (-a, -ur) *n. m.* male relative, uncle
frænk/a (-u, -ur) *n. f.* female relative, aunt
að fyrirgefa *v3* to forgive
fyrirgefðu *v2 imp.* sorry, forgive me
fyrst *adv.* first
fyrst/ur *adj.* first
föstudagskvöld (-s, –) *n. neu.* Friday evening
föstudag/ur (-s, -ar) *n. m.* Friday
föt *n. neu. (only in pl.)* clothes

gaffal/l (-s, gafflar) *n. m.* fork
gamal/l *adj.* old
gaman *n. neu.* fun
að ganga (ég geng) *v3* to walk
gat/a (götu, götur) *n. f.* street
að gefa *v3* to give

geisladisk/ur (-s, -ar) *n. m.* CD
geisladiskabúð (-ar, -ir) *n. f.* CD store
ger (-s, *) *n. neu.* yeast
að gera *v2* to do
gest/ur (-s, -ir) *n. m.* guest
að geta (ég get) *v3* to be able to
gift/ur *adj.* wedded, married
gjöf (gjafar, gjafir) *n. f.* gift, present
glað/ur (glöð *f.***)** *adj.* happy
glaðlynd/ur *adj.* happy (type of person)
glas (-s, glös) *n. neu.* glass
gleraugu *n. neu. (only in pl.)* glasses
að gleyma *v2* to forget
glugg/i (-a, -ar) *n. m.* window
golf (-s, *) *n. neu.* golf
góð/ur (góð *f.***, gott** *neu.***)** *adj.* good
grann/ur (grönn *f.***)** *adj.* slim
gras (-s, grös) *n. neu.* grass
grá/r (grátt *neu.***)** *adj.* gray
að grilla *v1* to barbecue
grín (-s, –) *n. neu.* joke
að grínast *v. st-form* to poke fun
græn/n *adj.* green
grænmeti (-s, *) *n. neu.* vegetable
grænmetisæt/a (-u, -ur) *n. f.* vegetarian
grænmetispíts/a (-u, -ur) *n. f.*
    vegetarian pizza
gul/ur *adj.* yellow
gæti *v. subj., see* **að geta**
gönguferð (-ar, -ir) *n. f.* walk, hiking

ha? *interj.* huh? what?
hamingjusam/ur (-söm *f.***)** *adj.* happy
hamborgar/i (-a, -ar) *n. m.* hamburger
hann *pron.* he, him
harðfisk/ur (-s, *) *n. m.* hardfish/dried
    fish, an Icelandic specialty
að hafa (ég hef) *v3* to have
að halda (ég held) *v3* to think, to give (a
    paper, a party)
handrit (-s, –) *n. neu.* manuscript
hangikjöt (-s, *) *n. neu.* smoked lamb,
    an Icelandic specialty
að hata *v1* to hate
hádegishlé (-s, –) *n. neu.* lunch break
hádegismat/ur (-ar, *) *n. m.* lunch

hálendi (-s, *) *n. neu.* highland
hálf/ur *adj.* half
há/r (hátt *neu.***)** *adj.* high, tall
hár (-s, –) *n. neu.* hair
háskól/i (-a, -ar) *n. m.* university
Háskól/i Íslands *n. masc. (nom.), n.*
    neu. (gen.) University of Iceland
að hefja (ég hef) *v3* to begin
heil/l *adj.* whole
heim *adv.* to home
heima *adv.* at home
heiman *adv.* from home
að heimsækja *v2* to visit
heimsókn (-ar, -ir) *n. f.* visit
að heita *v2* to be named
helg/i (-ar, -ar) *n. f.* weekend
hest/ur (-s, -ar) *n. m.* horse
heyrumst *v. st-form* we will talk later!
hér *adv.* here
hérna *adv.* here; also used as a
    hesitation marker
hingað *adv.* to here
að hitta *v2* to meet
að hittast *v. st-form* to meet each other
hjart/a (–, hjörtu) *n. neu.* heart
hjá *prep.* with, next to
að hjálpa *v1* to help
hjálpsam/ur (-söm *f.***)** *adj.* helpful
að hljóma *v1* to sound
hljómsveit (-ar, -ir) *n. f.* band
að hlusta *v1* to listen
hníf/ur (-s, -ar) *n. m.* knife
að horfa *v2* to watch
hrað/ur (hröð *f.***, hratt** *neu.***)** *adj.* fast
hress *adj.* healthy, in good spirits
að hringja *v2* to call, to phone
hring/ur (-s, -ir) *n. m.* ring, circle
hrædd/ur (hrætt *neu.***)** *adj.* scared
hugmynd (-ar, -ir) *n. f.* idea
hund/ur (-s, -ar) *n. m.* dog
húf/a (-u, -ur) *n. f.* hat
hún *pron.* she
hús (-s, –) *n. neu.* house
húsgagn (-s, -gögn) *n. neu.* furniture
hvað *pron.* what
hvaða *pron.* which

hvalaskoðun (-ar, *) *n. f.* whale watching
hval/ur (-s, ir) *n. m.* whale
hvar *adv.* where
hveiti (-s, *) *n. neu.* flour
hvenær *adv.* when
hver *pron.* who
hvernig *adv.* how
hvers vegna why?
hvít/ur *adj.* white
hægri *adj.* right (side)
hættu! *v. imp.* stop!
höfn (hafnar, hafnir) *n. f.* harbor
höfuðborg (-ar, -ir) *n. f.* capital city
höfuðborgarsvæði *n. neu.* Reykjavik and the surrounding area

inn *adv.* in
inni *adv.* inside

í *prep.* in
í kringum *prep.* around
íbúð (-ar, -ir) *n. f.* apartment
íbú/i (-a, -ar) *n. m.* inhabitant
ís (-s, -ar) *n. m.* ice, ice cream
íshokkí (-s, *) *n. neu.* ice hockey
Íslending/ur (-s, -ar) *n. m.* Icelander
íslensk/a (-u, *) *n. f.* Icelandic, referring to the language
íslensk/ur *adj.* Icelandic
ísskáp/ur (-s, -ar) *n. m.* refrigerator
íþrótt (-ar, -ir) *n. f.* sport

já *interj.* yes
jákvæð/ur (jákvætt *neu.)* *adj.* positive
jógúrt (-ar, *) *n. f.* or *neu.* yogurt
jú *interj.* yes (esp. after neg. questions)
jæja *interj.* well

kaffi (-s, *) *n. neu.* coffee
kaffihús (-s, –) *n. neu.* café
kaffistof/a (-u, -ur) *n. f.* common room at work
kallað/ur (kölluð *f.)* *adj.* called
Kanadamað/ur (-manns, -menn) *n. m.* Canadian (referring to people)

kannski *adv.* maybe
kass/i (-a, -ar) *n. m.* cash register, box
að kaupa *v2* to buy
kát/ur *adj.* happy
kennar/i (-a, -ar) *n. m.* teacher
kettling/ur (-s, -ar) *n. m.* kitten
að keyra *v2* to drive
kis/a (-u, -ur) *n. f.* cat (informal), kitty
að kíkja *v2* to have a look
kjúkling/ur (-s, -ar) *n. m.* chicken
kjöt (-s, *) *n. neu.* meat
að klæða sig *v2* to put on clothes
klósett (-s, –) *n. neu.* toilet, bathroom
klukk/a (-u, -ur) *n. f.* clock
klukkutím/i (-a, -ar) *n. m.* hour
kokk/ur (-s, -ar) *n. m.* cook
að koma (ég kem) *v3* to come
kommóð/a (-u, -ur) *n. f.* chest of drawers
kon/a (-u, ur) *n. f.* woman
kort (-s, –) *n. neu.* card (credit card, postcard, etc.), map
korter (-s, –) *n. neu.* quarter (of an hour)
að kosta *v1* to cost
kreditkort (-s, –) *n. neu.* credit card
krem (-s, –) *n. neu.* cream
krón/a (-u, -ur) *n. f.* krona, the Icelandic currency
kurteis *adj.* polite
að kveðja *v3* to say goodbye
kvöld (-s, –) *n. neu.* evening
að kynnast *v. st-form* to get to know
að kyssa *v2* to kiss
kærast/i (-a, -ar) *n. m.* boyfriend
kærast/a (-u, -ur) *n. f.* girlfriend
kött/ur (kattar, kettir) *n. m.* cat

að labba *v1* to walk (informal)
lag (-s, lög) *n. neu.* song
lambakjöt (-s, *) *n. neu.* lamb meat
lamp/i (-a, -ar) *n. m.* lamp
land (-s, lönd) *n. neu.* land, country
lang/ur (löng *f.)* *adj.* long
laugardagur (-s, -ar) *n. m.* Saturday
lauk/ur (-s, -ar) *n. m.* onion
laus *adj.* available

lat/ur (löt *f.*) *adj.* lazy
lán (-s, –) *n. neu.* loan
að lána *v1* to lend
leið (-ar, -ir) *n. f.* way
leiðinleg/ur *adj.* boring
leikar/i (-a, -ar) *n. m.* actor
leikrit (-s, –) *n. neu.* play (as in theater)
að lenda *v2* to land (in an airplane)
að leita *v1* to search
lengi *adv.* long (time)
lengur *adv. comp.* longer
að lifa *v2* to live
lifandi *adj.* live, alive
Listasafn Íslands National Gallery of
  Iceland
Listasafn Reykjavíkur Reykjavik Art
  Museum
að líða *v3 impersonal* to feel
líka *adv.* also
lítil/l (lítið *neu.*) *adj.* small, little
ljóð (-s, –) *n. neu.* poem
ljóshærð/ur *adj.* blond
ljósmynd (-ar, -ir) *n. f.* photograph
að lofa *v1* to promise
að loka *v1* to close
lund/i (-a, -ar) *n. m.* puffin
lung/a (-a, -u) *n. neu.* lung
lykil/l (-s, lyklar) *n. m.* key
að lýsa *v2* to describe
að læra *v2* to learn, to study
lögleg/ur *adj.* legal

mað/ur (manns, menn) *n. m.* man,
  husband
mamm/a (mömmu, mömmur) *n. f.*
  mom
manneskj/a (-u, -ur) *n. f.* person
mapp/a (möppu, möppur) *n. f.* binder
mat/ur (-ar, *) *n. m.* food
matseðil/l (-s, -seðlar) *n. m.* menu
mánudagur (-s, -ar) *n. m.* Monday
mánuð/ur (mánaðar, -ir) *n. m.* month
mega (ég má) *v. irr.* may
á meðan while
að meiða *v2* to hurt
meira *adv. comp.* more

meira að segja even
merkileg/ur *adj.* interesting
miðbæ/r (-jar, -ir) *n. m.* city center
mið/i (-a, -ar) *n. m.* ticket
miðvikudag/ur (-s, -ar) *n. m.*
  Wednesday
miðnætti (-s, *) *n. neu.* midnight
mikil/l (mikið *neu.*) *adj.* great
milli *prep.* between
minjagripabúð (-ar, -ir) *n. f.* souvenir
  shop
minni *adj. comp.* smaller
mínút/a (-u, -ur) *n. f.* minute
mjólk (-ur, *) *n. f.* milk
mjög *adv.* very
morgunmat/ur (-ar, *) *n. m.* breakfast
morgun/n (-s, morgnar) *n. m.* morning
  á morgun tomorrow
  í morgun this morning
móðurmál (-s, –) *n. neu.* mother tongue
að muna (ég man) *v. irr.* to remember
mynd (-ar, -ir) *n. f.* picture, painting,
  movie, photograph, image
myndarleg/ur *adj.* handsome
myndavél (-ar, -ar) *n. f.* camera
myndlistarmað/ur (-manns, -menn)
  n. m. artist (visual)
myndlistarsýning (-ar, -ar) *n. f.* art
  exhibit (visual)
að mæta *v2* to show up

nafn (-s, nöfn) *n. neu.* name
að ná (ég næ) *v5* to get, to reach, to fetch
nákvæmlega *adv.* exactly
nám (-s, *) *n. neu.* studies
náttborð (-s, –) *n. neu.* bedside table
náttúrulega *adv.* naturally, of course
að neðan *adv.* from below
nema *conj.* except
nemand/i (-a, nemendur) *n. m.* student
nesti (-s, *) *n. neu.* packed lunch,
  provisions
niðri *adv.* downstairs
niður *adv.* down
að njóta (ég nýt) *v3* to enjoy
norður (-s, *) *n. neu.* north

Norðurland (-s, *) *n. neu.* the north part
of Iceland
nóg *adv.* enough
nótt (nætur, nætur) *n. f.* night
nú *adv.* now
nú *interj.* oh
núna *adv.* now
ný/r (nýtt *neu.***)** *adj.* new
næst *adv.* next
næst/ur *adj.* next

of *adv.* too
að ofan *adv.* from above
ofboðslega *adv.* terribly
oft *adv.* often
oftast *adv. super.* usually
og *conj.* and
olí/a (-u, -ur) *n. f.* oil
að opna *v1* to open
orðabók (-ar, -bækur) *n. f.* dictionary
ostakak/a (-köku, -kökur) *n. f.*
cheesecake
ost/ur (-s, -ar) *n. m.* cheese

óábyrg/ur *adj.* irresponsible
óánægð/ur *adj.* disappointed
ódýr *adj.* inexpensive
ógift/ur *adj.* unmarried
ólögleg/ur *adj.* illegal
óskast *v. st-form* wanted
óvænt/ur *adj.* unexpected

pabb/i (-a, -ar) *n. m.* dad
að pakka *v1* to pack
pakk/i (-a, -ar) *n. m.* parcel
að panta *v1* to order
pappír (-s, -ar) *n. m.* paper, documents
pasta (–, *) *n. neu.* pasta
pening/ur (-s, -ar) *n. m.* money
penn/i (-a, -ar) *n. m.* pen
persón/a (-u, ur) *n. f.* person
peys/a (-u, -ur) *n. f.* sweater
pipar (-s, *) *n. m.* pepper
pína *n. f.* **(-u, *)** a bit
pínulítil/l *adj.* very small
píts/a (-u, -ur) *n. f.* pizza

plastpok/i (-a, -ar) *n. m.* plastic bag
póstkort (-s, –) *n. neu.* postcard
pöbb (-s, -ar) *n. m.* pub

rauð/ur (rautt *neu.***)** *adj.* red
rauðhærð/ur *adj.* with red hair,
redheaded
rauðvínsflask/a (-flösku, flöskur) *n. f.*
bottle of red wine
ráðstefn/a (-u, -ur) *n. f.* conference
regnbog/i (-a, -ar) *n. m.* rainbow
reiðufé (-fjár, *) *n. neu.* cash
að reykja *v2* to smoke
reykt/ur *adv.* smoked
að rétta *v2* to hand over
rétt/ur (-ar, -ir) *n. m.* dish, course
rithöfund/ur (-ar, -ar) *n. m.* author,
writer
rokk (-s, *) *n. neu.* rock (music)
rosalega *adv.* very, extremely
róleg/ur *adj.* relaxed, calm
rómantísk/ur *adj.* romantic
rúm (-s, –) *n. neu.* bed

sadd/ur (södd *f.***)** *adj.* full (after eating)
safn (-s, söfn) *n. neu.* museum
sag/a (sögu, sögur) *n. f.* story, history,
novel, saga
sagnfræði (–, *) *n. f.* history
sagnfræðing/ur (-s, -ar) *n. m.* historian
að sakna *v1* to miss
salat (-s, salöt) *n. neu.* salad
salt (-s, *) *n. neu.* salt
saman *adv.* together
samband (-s, -bönd) *n. neu.* connection,
contact, relationship
samlok/a (-u, -ur) *n. f.* sandwich
samt *adv.* still
sannarlega *adv.* truly
sálfræðing/ur (-s, -ar) *n. m.* psychologist
að segja *v2* to say
segðu mér *imp.* tell me
seinna *adv.* later
sem fyrst as soon as possible
sendand/i (-a, sendendur) *n. m.* sender
að sctja *v3* to put

að setjast *v3 st-form* to sit down
sé *v. irr. subj., see* **að vera**
séríslensk/ur *adj.* especially Icelandic
sérstaklega *adv.* especially
sérstak/ur (sérstök *f.*) *adj.* special
sig *personal pron. refl.* himself, herself, oneself
sigling (-ar, -ar) *n. f.* sailing
sinn *poss. pron. refl.* his, her, their
sím/i (-a, -ar) *n. m.* telephone
símanúmer (-s, –) *n. neu.* phone number
símtal (-s, símtöl) *n. neu.* phone call
sítrónuostakaka (-köku, -kökur) *n. f.* lemon cheesecake
að sjá (ég sé) *v5* to see
sjáðu! *v. imp.* look!
sjálf/ur *pron.* self
sjáumst *v5 st-form* see you!
sjopp/a (-u, -ur) *n. f.* convenience store
sjó/r (sjávar, *) *n. m.* sea, ocean
sjónvarp (-s, sjónvörp) *n. neu.* television
sjónvarpsherbergi (-s, –) *n. neu.* TV room
sjóveik/ur *adj.* seasick
skál (-ar, -ar) *n. f.* bowl
skál! *interj.* cheers!
skáld (-s, –) *n. neu.* writer, poet
skáldsag/a (-sögu, -sögur) *n. f.* novel
skeið (-ar, -ar) *n. f.* spoon
skemmtilegast/ur *adj. super.* most fun
skemmtileg/ur *adj.* fun, interesting
að skilja *v3* to understand, to depart, to divorce
skipti (-s, –) *n. neu.* times, occasions
skiptinem/i (-a, -ar) *n. m.* exchange student
sko *interj.* you see, well, certainly
að skoða *v1* to look at
skolhærð/ur *adj.* dirty blond, with light brown hair
skólatask/a (-tösku, -töskur) *n. f.* school bag
skól/i (-a, -ar) *n. m.* school
skó/r (-s, –) *n. m.* shoe
að skrifa *v1* to write

skrifborð (-s, –) *n. neu.* desk
skrifstof/a (-u, -ur) *n. f.* office
skulu (ég skal) *v. irr.* shall
skyr (-s, *) *n. neu.* skyr, an Icelandic milk product
skyrt/a (-u, -ur) *n. f.* shirt, blouse
skúff/a (-u, -ur) *n. f.* drawer
skýr *adj.* clear, smart
að slappa af *v1* to relax
að sleppa *v2* to skip
að smakka *v1* to taste
smá *adv.* a bit
smáræði (-s, –) *n. neu.* something small, a small gift
smjör (-s, *) *n. neu.* butter
að sofa (ég sef) *v3* to sleep
sofandi *adj.* sleeping
sokk/ur (-s, -ar) *n. m.* sock
son/ur (-ar, synir) *n. m.* son
sófaborð (-s, –) *n. neu.* coffee table
sóf/i (-a, -ar) *n. m.* sofa
sól (-ar, ir) *n. f.* sun
spennandi *adj.* exciting
spennt/ur *adj.* excited
að spila *v1* to play
spurning (-ar, -ar) *n. f.* question
stadd/ur (stödd *f.*) *adj.* located
að standa (ég stend) *v3* to stand, to be written
starf (-s, störf) *n. neu.* work
starfsmað/ur (-manns, -menn) *n. m.* employee
stein/n (-s, -ar) *n. m.* stone
stelp/a (-u, -ur) *n. f.* girl
steinsofandi *adj.* sleeping very deeply
stof/a (-u, -ur) *n. f.* living room
stofuborð (-s, –) *n. neu.* coffee table
stól/l (-s, -ar) *n. m.* chair
stór *adj.* big
strák/ur (-s, -ar) *n. m.* boy
strætó (-s, -ar) *n. m.* bus
stundum *adv.* sometimes
sturt/a (-u, -ur) *n. f.* shower
suður (-s, *) *n. neu.* south
Suðurland (-s, *) *n. neu.* the south part of Iceland

sumar (-s, sumur) *n. neu.* summer
sund (-s, *) *n. neu.* swimming
sundlaug (-ar, -ar) *n. f.* swimming pool
sunnudag/ur (-s, -ar) *n. m.* Sunday
súkkulaði (-s, –) *n. neu.* chocolate
súp/a (-u, -ur) *n. f.* soup
súpupakk/i (-a, -ar) *n. m.* instant soup
svakalega *adv.* enormously, extremely
svang/ur (svöng f.) *adj.* hungry
að svara *v1* to answer
svart/ur (svört f.) *adj.* black
svefnherbergi (-s, –) *n. neu.* bedroom
svefnpok/i (-a, -ar) *n. m.* sleeping bag
sveit (-ar, -ir) *n. f.* rural area
svipað/ur (svipuð f.) *adj.* similar
svo *adv.* so, then
sykur (-s, *) *n. m.* sugar
sykurlaus *adj.* sugarfree
systir (systur, systur) *n. f.* sister
að sýna *v2* to show
að sýnast *v2 st-form* to seem
sýning (-ar, -ar) *n. f.* show
sæl/l *adj.* hi! (*lit.* happy)
sæti (-s, –) *n. neu.* seat
sæt/ur *adj.* sweet, cute
sömuleiðis *adv.* likewise
söngvar/i (-a, -ar) *n. m.* singer

að taka (ég tek) *v3* to take
að tala *v1* to speak
tannburst/i (-a, -ar) *n. m.* toothbrush
task/a (tösku, töskur) *n. f.* bag, purse
að telja *v3* to count
til dæmis for example
tilbúin/n (tilbúið *neu.*) *adj.* ready
tím/i (-a, -ar) *n. m.* time, class
tjald (-s, tjöld) *n. neu.* tent
að tjalda *v1* to go camping
tjaldstæði (-s, –) *n. neu.* camping site
tómat/ur (-s, -ar) *n. m.* tomato
tómatsós/a (-u, -ur) *n. f.* ketchup, tomato sauce
tónleik/ar *n. f. pl.* concert
tónlist (-ar, *) *n. f.* music
trefil/l (-s, treflar) *n. m.* scarf
tungumál (-s, –) *n. neu.* language

túnfisksdós (-ar, ir) *n. f.* tin of tuna
tvisvar *adv.* twice
að týna *v2* to lose
tölv/a (-u, -ur) *n. f.* computer
tölvutónlist (-ar, *) *n. f.* electronic music

um *prep.* around, about
undir *prep.* under
upp *adv.* up
uppalin/n *adj.* raised
uppi *adv.* upstairs
upptekin/n *adj.* busy, occupied, in use

úlp/a (-u, -ur) *n. f.* winter jacket
út *adv.* out
að útbúa (ég útbý) *v5* to prepare
úti *adv.* outside
útileg/a (-u, -ur) *n. f.* camping
útvarp (-s, útvörp) *n. neu.* radio

að vakna *v1* to wake up
vandamál (-s, –) *n. neu.* problem
að vanta *v1 impersonal* to lack
var *v. irr. past, see* **að vera**
vara (vöru, vörur) *n. f.* goods
vask/ur (-s, -ar) *n. m.* sink
að vaska upp *v1* to do the dishes
vatn (-s, vötn) *n. neu.* water, lake
vá! *interj.* wow!
vegabréf (-s, –) *n. neu.* passport
veik/ur *adj.* sick
veisl/a (-u, -ur) *n. f.* party
veitingastað/ur (-ar, -ir) *n. m.* restaurant
vel *adv.* well, good
venjulega *adv.* usually
venjuleg/ur *adj.* ordinary
að vera *v. irr.* to be
    að vera hægt to be possible
    að vera með to have, to own
    að vera orðin/n to have become
    að vera til to exist, to be available
verða *v3* to become, to have to
veski (-s, –) *n. neu.* wallet
vesti (-s, –) *n. neu.* vest
vestur (-s, *) *n. neu.* west

Vestfirðir *n. m. pl.* the Icelandic west
    fjords
Vesturland (-s, *) *n. neu.* the western
    part of Iceland
vettling/ur (-s, -ar) *n. m.* mitten
við *pron.* we
við *prep.* at, by
viðkvæm/ur *adj.* sensitive
viðtal (-s, -töl) *n. neu.* interview
vik/a (-u, -ur) *n. f.* week
að vilja (ég vil) *v. irr.* to want
vinkon/a (-u, -ur) *n. f.* friend
    (female)
að vinna *v3* to work
vinn/a (-u, -ur) *n. f.* work
vinsæl/l *adj.* popular
vinsamlegast *adv.* kindly
vinstri *adj.* left
vind/ur (-s, -ar) *n. m.* wind
vin/ur (-ar, -ir) *n. m.* friend

það *pron.* it
þangað *adv.* to there
þar *adv.* there
þarna *adv.* over there
þau *pron. neu. pl.* they
þá *adv.* then
þeir *pron. m. pl.* they
þessi (þetta *neu.***)** *pron.* this
þegiðu! *v. imp.* shush!
þetta *pron. neu.*, see **þessi**

þið *pron. pl.* you (pl.)
Þjóðmenningarhúsið *n. neu. def.* The
    Culture House
Þjóðminjasafnið *n. neu. def.* The
    National Museum
þjón/n (-s, -ar) *n. m.* waiter
þreytt/ur *adj.* tired
þriðjudagur (-s, -ar) *n. m.* Tuesday
þungarokk (-s, *) *n. neu.* heavy metal
að þurfa (ég þarf) *v. irr.* to need
þú *pron.* you (sing.)
þúsund (-s, –) *n. neu.* thousand
því *pron. neu./dat.* it
því *conj.* because
þvottahús (-s, –) *n. neu.* laundry room
þvottavél (-ar, -ar) *n. f.* washing
    machine
þýsk/a (-u, *) *n. f.* German, referring to
    the language
Þýskaland (-s, *) *n. neu.* Germany
þær *pron. f. pl.* they

æi! *interj.* oh (no)!
æðislega *adv.* madly, awfully
    æðislega gott terribly good
að æfa *v2* to practice, to rehearse
æfing (-ar, -ar) *n. f.* exercise, rehearsal,
    practice
að ætla *v1* to intend

öruggara *adv. comp.* safer

ENGLISH-ICELANDIC GLOSSARY

For grammatical information on the Icelandic words, see the Icelandic-English glossary.

a bit *adv.* aðeins, dálítið, pínu, smá
about *prep.* um
actor *n.* leikar/i
actually *adv.* eiginlega
advertisement *n.* auglýsing
after *prep.* eftir
again *adv.* aftur
airplane *n.* flugvél
all *pron.* all/ur
almost *adv.* eiginlega
alone *adj.* ein/n, einsamal/l
also *adv.* líka
always *adv.* alltaf
American *adj.* amerísk/ur, bandarísk/ur
American *n.* Ameríkan/i
and *conj.* og
another *pron.* annar
to answer *v.* að svara
anything *pron.* neitt
apartment *n.* íbúð
apple *n.* epli
around *adv.* í kringum, um
art exhibit (visual) *n.* myndlistarsýning
artist (visual) *n.* myndlistarmað/ur
at *prep.* við, hjá
author *n.* rithöfundur
available *adj.* laus, að vera við
awfully *adv.* æðislega, rosalega

backpack *n.* bakpok/i
bag *n.* task/a
to bake *v.* að baka
banana *n.* banan/i
band *n.* hljómsveit
to barbecue *v.* að grilla

bath tub *n.* baðker
bathroom *n.* baðherbergi
to be *v.* að vera
to be able *v.* að geta
beautiful *adj.* falleg/ur
because *conj.* því, af því að
to become *v.* að verða
bed *n.* rúm
bedside table *n.* náttborð
bedroom *n.* svefnherbergi
beer *n.* bjór
before *prep.* áður
to begin *v.* að hefja, að byrja
belt *n.* belti
best *adj. super.* best/ur
between *prep.* milli
big *adj.* stór
binder *n.* mapp/a
birthday *n.* afmæli
birthday party *n.* afmælisveisl/a
birthday present *n.* afmælisgjöf
black *adj.* svart/ur
blond *adj.* ljóshærð/ur
blue *adj.* blá/r
boat *n.* bát/ur
book *n.* bók
boring *adj.* leiðinleg/ur
both *pron.* báðir
bottle of red wine *n.* rauðvínsflask/a
bowl *n.* skál
boy *n.* strák/ur
boyfriend *n.* kærast/i
bread *n.* brauð
breakfast *n.* morgunmat/ur
bright *adj.* bjart/ur

broke *adj.* blank/ur
brother *n.* bróðir
brown *adj.* brún/n
bus *n.* strætó
busy *adj.* upptekin/n
but *conj.* en
butter *n.* smjör
to buy *v.* að kaupa
by *prep.* eftir, við
bye! *interj.* bæ! (informal)

café *n.* kaffihús
to call *v.* að hringja
camera *n.* myndavél
to camp *v.* að tjalda
camping *n.* útileg/a
camping site *n.* tjaldstæði
Canadian *n.* Kanadamað/ur
capital city *n.* höfuðborg
car *n.* bíl/l
car key *n.* bíllykil/l
card *n.* kort
to carry *v.* að bera
cash *n.* reiðufé
cash register *n.* kass/i
cat *n.* kött/ur, kisa (informal)
CD *n.* geisladisk/ur
CD store *n.* geisladiskabúð
cell phone *n.* farsím/i
chair *n.* stól/l
to check *v.* að athuga
cheers! *interj.* skál!
cheese *n.* ost/ur
cheesecake *n.* ostakak/a
chest of drawers *n.* kommóð/a
chicken *n.* kjúkling/ur
child *n.* barn
chocolate *n.* súkkulaði
city *n.* borg
city center *n.* miðbæ/r
class *n.* tím/i
clear *adj.* skýr
clock *n.* klukk/a
to close *v.* að loka
clothes *n.* föt (*only pl.*)
clothing store *n.* fatabúð

coffee *n.* kaffi
coffee table *n.* sófaborð
to come *v.* að koma
completely *adv.* alveg
computer *n.* tölv/a
conference *n.* ráðstefn/a
connection *n.* samband
convenience store *n.* sjopp/a
to cook *v.* að elda
cook *n.* kokk/ur
cool! *adv.* flott!
to cost *v.* að kosta
to count *v.* að telja
counter *n.* búðarborð
country *n.* land
credit card *n.* kreditkort
cream *n.* krem (lotion), rjómi (dairy product)

dad *n.* pabb/i
Danish (language) *n.* dansk/a
Danish *adj.* dansk/ur
darling *n.* elsk/a
daughter *n.* dóttir
day *n.* dag/ur
to decide *v.* að ákveða
den *n.* sjónvarpsherbergi
to describe *v.* að lýsa
desk *n.* skrifborð
dessert *n.* eftirrétt/ur
dictionary *n.* orðabók
difficult *adj.* erfið/ur
diligent *adj.* dugleg/ur
dining room *n.* borðstofa
dirty blond *adj.* skolhærð/ur
disappointed *adj.* óánægð/ur
dish *n.* rétt/ur
to do *v.* að gera
to do the dishes *v.* að vaska upp
dog *n.* hund/ur
dollar *n.* dollar/i
down *adv.* niður
downstairs *adv.* niðri
downtown *n.* miðbæ/r
drawer *n.* skúff/a
to dream *v.* að dreyma

to drink *v.* að drekka
to drive *v.* að keyra
drop *n.* drop/i

ear *n.* eyr/a
east *n.* austur, Austurland
to eat *v.* að borða
either ... or *conj.* annað hvort ... eða
electronic music *n.* tölvutónlist, raftónlist
employee *n.* starfsmað/ur
English (language) *n.* ensk/a
English *adj.* ensk/ur
to enjoy *v.* að njóta
enormously *adv.* svakalega, ofsalega, rosalega
enough *adv.* nóg
entire *adj.* all/ur
entrance hall *n.* forstof/a
especially *adv.* sérstaklega
eternity *n.* eilífð
even *adv.* meira að segja
evening *n.* kvöld
everyday *adv.* á hverjum degi
everywhere *adv.* alls staðar
exactly *adv.* einmitt, nákvæmlega
except *adv.* nema
exchange student *n.* skiptinem/i
excited *adj.* spennt/ur
exciting *adj.* spennandi
to excuse *v.* að afsaka
exercise *n.* æfing
to exist *v.* að vera til
expensive *adj.* dýr
extremely *adv.* rosalega, ofsalega, svakalega
eye *n.* aug/a

fast *adj.* hrað/ur
fast *adv.* hratt
to feel *v.* að líða
to fetch *v.* að ná í
finished *adj.* búin/n
first *adv.* fyrst
fish *n.* fisk/ur
fjord *n.* fjörð/ur

flour *n.* hveiti
flower *n.* blóm
food *n.* mat/ur
for example til dæmis
to forget *v.* að gleyma
to forgive *v.* að fyrirgefa
fork *n.* gaffal/l
French (language) *n.* fransk/a
French *adj.* fransk/ur
french fries *n.* franskar kartöflur
Friday *n.* föstudag/ur
Friday evening *n.* föstudagskvöld
friend *n.* vin/ur, vinkon/a (female)
full *adj.* sadd/ur (after eating)
fun *adj.* skemmtileg/ur
fun *n.* gaman
furniture *n.* húsgagn

German (language) *n.* þýsk/a
Germany *n.* Þýskaland
to get *v.* að fá
to get to know *v.* að kynnast
gift *n.* gjöf
girl *n.* stelp/a
girlfriend *n.* kærast/a
to give *v.* að gefa
glass *n.* glas
glasses *n.* gleraugu
to go *v.* að fara
to go horseback riding *v.* að fara á hestbak
golf *n.* golf
good *adj.* góð/ur
goodbye *interj.* bless, sjáumst, heyrumst, bæ
goods *n.* vara
grandfather *n.* af/i
grandmother *n.* amm/a
grass *n.* gras
gray *adj.* grá/r
great *adj.* frábær, mikil/l
green *adj.* græn/n
guest *n.* gest/ur

hair *n.* hár
half *adj.* hálf/ur

hamburger *n.* hamborgar/i
to hand over *v.* að rétta
handsome *adj.* myndarleg/ur
happy *adj.* glað/ur, hamingjusam/ur,
    kát/ur, hress
harbor *n.* höfn
hat *n.* húf/a
to hate *v.* að hata
to have *v.* að hafa, að eiga, að vera með
to have a look *v.* að kíkja
to hold a premier *v.* að frumsýna
he *pron.* hann
heart *n.* hjart/a
heavy metal (music) *n.* þungarokk
to help *v.* að hjálpa
helpful *adj.* hjálpsam/ur
her *pron.* hana *(acc.)*, henni *(dat.)*,
    hennar *(gen.)*
here *adv.* hér, hérna (here), hingað (to
    here), héðan (from here)
hi! *interj.* blessað/ur!, sæl/l!, hæ!, halló!
high *adj.* há/r
highland *n.* hálendi
him *pron.* hann *(acc.)*, honum *(dat.)*,
    hans *(gen.)*
historian *n.* sagnfræðing/ur
history *n.* sagnfræði
home *adv.* heim (to home), heima (at
    home), heiman (from home)
horse *n.* hest/ur
hour *n.* klukkutím/i
house *n.* hús
how *adv.* hvernig
huh? *interj.* ha?
hungry *adj.* svang/ur
to hurry up *v.* að drífa sig
to hurt *v.* að meiða

I *pron.* ég *(nom.)*
ice cream *n.* ís
ice hockey *n.* íshokkí
Icelander *n.* Íslending/ur
Icelandic (language) *n.* íslensk/a
Icelandic *adj.* íslensk/ur
idea *n.* hugmynd

if *conj.* ef
illegal *adj.* ólögleg/ur
in *adv.* inn (movement), inni (location)
in *prep.* í
individual *n.* einstakling/ur
inexpensive *adj.* ódýr
inhabitant *n.* íbú/i
inside *adv.* inni
instant soup *n.* súpupakk/i
to intend *v.* að ætla
interest *n.* áhug/i, áhugamál
interesting *adj.* áhugaverð/ur,
    merkileg/ur
interview *n.* viðtal
to invite *v.* að bjóða
irresponsible *adj.* óábyrg/ur
it *pron.* það *(nom. and acc.)*, því *(dat.)*,
    þess *(gen.)*

jazz *n.* djass
journalist *n.* blaðamað/ur
just *adv.* bara

ketchup *n.* tómatsós/a
key *n.* lykil/l
kindly *adv.* vinsamlegast
to kiss *v.* að kyssa
kitchen *n.* eldhús
kitchen chair *n.* eldhússtól/l
kitchen table *n.* eldhúsborð
kitten *n.* kettling/ur
knife *n.* hníf/ur

to lack *v.* að vanta
lamb meat *n.* lambakjöt
lamp *n.* lamp/i
to land *v.* að lenda
land *n.* land
language *n.* tungumál
laptop *n.* fartölv/a
later *adv.* seinna, síðar
laundry room *n.* þvottahús
lazy *adj.* lat/ur
to learn *v.* að læra
left *adj* vinstri

legal *adj.* lögleg/ur
lemon cheesecake *n.* sítrónuostakak/a
to lend *v.* að lána
likewise *adv.* sömuleiðis
to listen *v.* að hlusta
literature *n.* bókmenntir *(only pl.)*
to live *v.* að búa, að lifa
live music lifandi tónlist
living room *n.* stof/a
loan *n.* lán
located *adj.* stadd/ur
long *adj.* lang/ur
long *adv.* (duration) lengi
longer *adv.* lengur
to look at *v.* að skoða
look! *interj.* sjáðu!, sko!
to lose *v.* að týna
love *n.* ást
to love *v.* að elska
lunch *n.* hádegismat/ur
lunch break *n.* hádegishlé
lung *n.* lung/a

madly *adv.* æðislega
man *n.* mað/ur
manuscript *n.* handrit
map *n.* kort, landakort
married *adj.* gift/ur
match *n.* eldspýt/a
mattress *n.* dýn/a
may *v.* að mega
maybe *adv.* kannski
me *pron.* mig *(acc.)*, mér *(dat.)*, mín *(gen.)*
meat *n.* kjöt
to meet *v.* að hitta, að hittast, að mæta
menu *n.* matseðil/l
midnight *n.* miðnætti
milk *n.* mjólk
minute *n.* mínút/a
to miss *v.* að sakna
mitten *n.* vettling/ur
mom *n.* mamm/a
Monday *n.* mánudagur
money *n.* pening/ur
month *n.* mánuð/ur
more *adj.* fleira, meira

morning *n.* morgun/n
mother tongue *n.* móðurmál
movie *n.* (bíó)mynd, (kvik)mynd
movie theater *n.* bíó, kvikmyndahús
museum *n.* safn
music *n.* tónlist

name *n.* nafn
naturally *adv.* náttúrulega
necktie *n.* bindi
to need *v.* að þurfa
new *adj.* ný/r
next *adv.* næst
next *adj.* næst/ur
nice *adj.* ágæt/ur
night *n.* nótt
no one *pron.* engin/n
no problem ekkert mál
north *n.* norður, Norðurland
not *adv.* ekki
nothing *adv.* ekkert
novel *n.* skáldsag/a
now *adv.* nú, núna

ocean *n.* sjó/r
of *prep.* af
of course *adv.* auðvitað
office *n.* skrifstof/a
often *adv.* oft
oh (no)! *interj.* æ!, æi!
oil *n.* olí/a
old *adj.* gamal/l
on *prep.* á
once *adv.* einu sinni
one *num.* ein/n
one moment augnablik
oneself *pron.* sig *(acc.)*, sér *(dat.)*, sín *(gen.)*
onion *n.* lauk/ur
to open *v.* að opna
orange *n.* appelsín/a
orange *adj.* appelsínugul/ur
orange juice *n.* appelsínusaf/i
to order *v.* að panta
ordinary *adj.* venjuleg/ur
out *adv.* út

outside *adv.* úti
oven *n.* bakaraofn
over there *adv.* þarna

to pack *v.* að pakka
packed lunch *n.* nesti
painting *n.* mynd, málverk
paper *n.* pappír
**paper (an academic paper given at a
    lecture)** *n.* erindi
parcel *n.* pakk/i
parent *n.* foreldri *neu. sing.*,
    foreldrar *m. pl.*
party *n.* veisl/a, partí
passport *n.* vegabréf, pass/i
pasta *n.* pasta
to pay *v.* að borga
peace *n.* frið/ur
pen *n.* penn/i
people *n.* fólk *(only sing.)*
pepper *n.* pipar, paprika (sweet pepper)
person *n.* persón/a, manneskj/a
phone call *n.* símtal
phone number *n.* símanúmer
photograph *n.* ljósmynd
picture *n.* mynd
pineapple *n.* ananas
pink *adj.* bleik/ur
pizza *n.* píts/a
plane ticket *n.* flugmið/i
plastic bag *n.* plastpok/i
plate *n.* disk/ur
to play *v.* að spila
play (as in theater) *n.* leikrit
pleased *adj.* ánægð/ur
poem *n.* ljóð
poet *n.* skáld
polite *adj.* kurteis
popular *adj.* vinsæl/l
positive *adj.* jákvæð/ur
to be possible *v.* að vera hægt
postcard *n.* póstkort
to practise *v.* að æfa
premier *n.* frumsýning
to prepare *v.* að útbúa
problem *n.* vandamál

to promise *v.* að lofa
psychologist *n.* sálfræðing/ur
pub *n.* pöbb
puffin *n.* lund/i
purple *adj.* fjólublá/r
to put *v.* að setja

quarter (of an hour) *n.* korter
question *n.* spurning

radio *n.* útvarp
rainbow *n.* regnbog/i
raised *adj.* uppalin/n
rather *adv.* frekar
ready *adj.* tilbúin/n
red *adj.* rauð/ur
refrigerator *n.* ísskáp/ur
to rehearse *v.* að æfa
rehearsal *n.* æfing
relative *n.* frænk/a *(female)*, frænd/i
    (male)
to relax *v.* að slappa af
relaxed *adj.* róleg/ur
to remember *v.* að muna
reserved *adj.* frátekin/n
responsible *adj.* ábyrg/ur
restaurant *n.* veitingastað/ur
right *adj.* hægri (direction),
    rétt/ur (correct)
ring *n.* hring/ur
rock (music) *n.* rokk
romantic *adj.* rómantísk/ur
rural area *n.* sveit

safer *adj. comp.* öruggara
sailing *n.* sigling
salad *n.* salat
salt *n.* salt
sandwich *n.* samlok/a
Saturday *n.* laugardag/ur
to say *v.* að segja
scared *adj.* hrædd/ur
scarf *n.* trefil/l
school *n.* skól/i
school bag *n.* skólatask/a
to search *v.* að leita

seasick *adj.* sjóveik/ur
seat *n.* sæti
second serving *n.* ábót
to see *v.* að sjá
see you! sjáumst!
to seem *v.* að sýnast, að virðast
self *pron.* sjálf/ur
sender *n.* sendand/i
sensitive *adj.* viðkvæm/ur
serious *adj.* alvörugefin/n
shall *v.* skulu
she *pron.* hún *(nom.)*, hana *(acc.)*,
    henni *(dat.)*, hennar *(gen.)*
shirt *n.* skyrt/a
shoe *n.* skó/r
shop *n.* búð
to show *v.* að sýna
show *n.* sýning
shower *n.* sturt/a
shush! *interj.* uss!, þegiðu!
shy *adj.* feimin/n
sick *adj.* veik/ur
similar *adj.* svipað/ur
singer *n.* söngvar/i
sink *n.* vask/ur
sister *n.* systir
to sit down *v.* að setjast
to skip *v.* að sleppa
to sleep *v.* að sofa
sleeping *adj.* sofandi
sleeping bag *n.* svefnpok/i
slim *adj.* grann/ur
small *adj.* lítil/l
smaller *adj. comp.* minni
smart *adj.* klár, gáfað/ur
to smoke *v.* að reykja
smoked *adj.* reykt/ur
so *adv.* svo
soccer *n.* fótbolt/i
sock *n.* sokk/ur
sofa *n.* sóf/i
something *pron.* eitthvað
sometimes *adv.* stundum
son *n.* son/ur
song *n.* lag
soon *adv.* bráðum

sorry! *imp.* fyrirgefðu! *sing.*, fyrirgefið *pl.*
to sound *v.* að hljóma
soup *n.* súp/a
south *n.* suður, Suðurland
souvenir shop *n.* minjagripabúð
to speak *v.* að tala
special *adj.* sérstak/ur
spoon *n.* skeið
sport *n.* íþrótt
to start *v.* að byrja
still *adv.* enn, samt
stone *n.* stein/n
story *n.* sag/a
street *n.* gat/a
student *n.* nemand/i
studies *n.* nám
to study *v.* að læra
stuff *n.* dót
sugar *n.* sykur
sugarfree *adj.* sykurlaus
summer *n.* sumar
sun *n.* sól
Sunday *n.* sunnudag/ur
surely *adv.* ábyggilega
sweater *n.* peys/a
sweet *adj.* sæt/ur
swimming *n.* sund
swimming pool *n.* sundlaug

table *n.* borð
to take *v.* að taka
to take a shower *v.* að fara í sturtu
tall *adj.* há/r
to taste *v.* að smakka
teacher *n.* kennar/i
telephone *n.* sím/i
television *n.* sjónvarp
tent *n.* tjald
terribly *adv.* ofboðslega
then *adv.* þá, svo
there *adv.* þar, þangað (to there),
    þaðan (from there)
they *pron.* þeir *m.*, þær *f.*, þau *neu.*
to think *v.* að halda, að hugsa, að finnast
this *pron.* þetta *neu.*, þessi *m. and f.*
thousand *n.* þúsund

Thursday *n.* fimmtudag/ur
ticket *n.* mið/i
time *n.* tím/i
tin *n.* dós
tired *adj.* þreytt/ur
together *adv.* saman
tomato *n.* tómat/ur
tomato sauce *n.* tómatsós/a
tomorrow *adv.* á morgun
too *adv.* of, líka
toothbrush *n.* tannburst/i
tour *n.* ferðalag
tourist *n.* ferðamað/ur
town *n.* bæ/r
trip *n.* ferð
truly *adv.* sannarlega
Tuesday *n.* þriðjudag/ur
TV room (den) *n.* sjónvarpsherbergi
twice *adv.* tvisvar

under *prep.* undir
to understand *v.* að skilja
unexpected *adj.* óvænt/ur
university *n.* háskól/i
University of Iceland *n.* Háskóli
    Íslands
unmarried *adj.* ógift/ur
up *adv.* upp
upstairs *adv.* uppi
USA *n.* Bandaríkin
usually *adv.* oftast

vacation *n.* frí
vegetable *n.* grænmeti
vegetarian *n.* grænmetisæt/a
vegetarian pizza *n.* grænmetispíts/a
very *adv.* mjög, rosalega
vest *n.* vesti
visit *n.* heimsókn
to visit *v.* að heimsækja

wait! *v. imp.* bíddu!
waiter *n.* þjón/n
to wake up *v.* að vakna
to walk *v.* að ganga, að labba *(informal)*

walk *n.* gönguferð
wallet *n.* veski
to want *v.* að vilja
washing machine *n.* þvottavél
to watch *v.* að horfa
water *n.* vatn
way *n.* leið
we *pron.* við *(nom.)*, okkur *(acc. and*
    dat.), okkar *(gen.)*
Wednesday *n.* miðvikudag/ur
week *n.* vik/a
weekend *n.* helg/i
well *adv.* vel
well *interj.* sko, jæja
west *n.* vestur
whale *n.* hval/ur
whale watching *n.* hvalaskoðun
what *adv.* hvað
when *adv.* hvenær
where *adv.* hvar
which *adv.* hvaða
while *conj.* á meðan
white *adj.* hvít/ur
who *pron.* hver
whole *adj.* all/ur (öll *f.*), heil/l
why *adv.* af hverju, hvers vegna
wind *n.* vind/ur
window *n.* glugg/i
winter jacket *n.* úlp/a
woman *n.* kon/a
to work *v.* að vinna
work *n.* vinn/a, starf
wow! *interj.* vá!
write *v.* að skrifa
writer *n.* rithöfund/ur

yeast *n.* ger
yellow *adj.* gul/ur
yes *interj.* já, jú (after negative
    questions)
yogurt *n.* jógúrt
you *pron. sing.* þú *(nom.)*, þig *(acc.)*,
    þér *(dat.)*, þín *(gen.)*
you *pron. pl.* þið *(nom.)*, ykkur *(acc.*
    and dat.), ykkar *(gen.)*

CD Track List

Disc 1

1. The Icelandic Alphabet, p. 7
2. Special Letter Combinations, p. 10
3. Pronunciation of vowels before *ng* and *nk*, p. 10
4. Double Consonants, p. 11
5. Stress, p. 12
6. Length of Vowels, p. 13
7. Les. 1: Samtal 1, p. 16
8. Les. 1: Samtal 1 for repetition, p. 16
9. Les. 1: Orðaforði, p. 20
10. Les. 1: Orðasambönd, p. 21
11. Les. 2: Samtal, p. 28
12. Les. 2: Samtal for repetition, p. 28
13. Les. 2: Orðaforði, p. 30
14. Les. 2: Orðasambönd, p. 30
15. Les. 3: Samtal, p. 36
16. Les. 3: Samtal for repetition, p. 36
17. Les. 3: Orðaforði, p. 38
18. Les. 3: Orðasambönd, p. 38
19. Les. 4: Samtal 1, p. 46
20. Les. 4: Samtal 1 for repetition, p. 46
21. Les. 4: Orðaforði, p. 50
22. Les. 4: Names of countries, p. 50
23. Les. 4: Colors, p. 55
24. Les. 5: Samtal 1, p. 60
25. Les. 5: Samtal 1 for repetition, p. 60
26. Les. 5: Orðaforði, p. 64
27. Les. 5: Orðasambönd, p. 64
28. Les. 5: Numbers 1–20, p. 67
29. Les. 6: Samtal, p. 74
30. Les. 6: Samtal for repetition, p. 74
31. Les. 6: Orðaforði, p. 76
32. Les. 6: Days of the week, p. 76
33. Les. 7: Samtal, p. 88
34. Les. 7: Samtal for repetition, p. 88
35. Les. 7: Orðaforði, p. 92
36. Les. 7: Orðasambönd, p. 92

Disc 2

1. Les. 8: Samtal 1, p. 102
2. Les. 8: Samtal 1 for repetition, p. 102
3. Les. 8: Orðaforði, p. 106
4. Les. 8: Orðasambönd, p. 106
5. Les. 9: Samtal 1, p. 114
6. Les. 9: Samtal 1 for repetition, p. 114
7. Les. 9: Orðaforði, p. 118
8. Les. 9: Orðasambönd, p. 118
9. Les. 10: Samtal 1, p. 130
10. Les. 10: Samtal 1 for repetition, p. 130
11. Les. 10: Orðaforði, p. 134
12. Les. 10: Orðasambönd, p. 134
13. Les. 11: Samtal, p. 146
14. Les. 11: Samtal for repetition, p. 146
15. Les. 11: Orðaforði, p. 150
16. Les. 11: Orðasambönd, p. 150
17. Les. 12: Samtal, p. 160
18. Les. 12: Samtal for repetition, p. 160
19. Les. 12: Orðaforði, p. 162
20. Les. 13: Samtal, p. 168
21. Les. 13: Samtal for repetition, p. 168
22. Les. 13: Orðaforði, p. 170
23. Les. 13: Orðasambönd, p. 170
24. Les. 14: Samtal, p. 178
25. Les. 14: Samtal for repetition, p. 178
26. Les. 14: Orðaforði, p. 182
27. Les. 14: Orðasambönd, p. 182

Scandinavian-Interest Titles from Hippocrene Books

Beginner's Danish with 2 Audio CDs
ISBN 978-0-7818-1199-6 · $35.00pb

Danish-English/English-Danish Practical Dictionary
32,000 entries · ISBN 0-87052-823-8 · $16.95pb

Beginner's Finnish with 2 Audio CDs
ISBN 978-0-7818-1228-3 · $32.00pb

Finnish-English/English-Finnish Concise Dictionary
12,000 entries · ISBN 0-87052-813-0 · $14.95pb

Finnish-English/English-Finnish Dictionary & Phrasebook
5,000 entries · ISBN 0-7818-0956-8 · $14.95pb

Icelandic-English/English-Icelandic Concise Dictionary
10,000 entries · ISBN 0-87052-801-7 · $14.95pb

Beginner's Norwegian with 2 Audio CDs, Second Edition
ISBN 978-0-78181299-3 · $32.00pb

Hippocrene Children's Illustrated Norwegian Dictionary
500 entries · ISBN 0-7818-0887-3 · $14.95pb

Norwegian-English/English-Norwegian Practical Dictionary
50,000 entries · ISBN 978-0-7818-1106-4 · $27.50pb

Norwegian-English/English-Norwegian Dictionary & Phrasebook
3,500 entries · ISBN 0-7818-0955-X · $14.95pb

Beginner's Swedish with 2 Audio CDs
ISBN 0-7818-1157-0 · $32.00pb

Swedish-English/English-Swedish Practical Dictionary
28,000 entries · ISBN 978-0-7818-1246-7 · $29.95pb

Hippocrene Children's Illustrated Swedish Dictionary
500 entries · ISBN 0-7818-0850-7 · $14.95pb

Swedish-English/English-Swedish Dictionary & Phrasebook
3,000 entries · ISBN 0-7818-0903-7 · $11.95pb

Prices subject to change without prior notice. **To purchase Hippocrene Books** contact your local bookstore, visit www.hippocrenebooks.com, call (212) 685-4373, or write to: HIPPOCRENE BOOKS, 171 Madison Avenue, New York, NY 10016.